3 SPECIAL EDUCATION IN TRANSITION

Administrator's Handbook on Integrating America's Mildly Handicapped Students

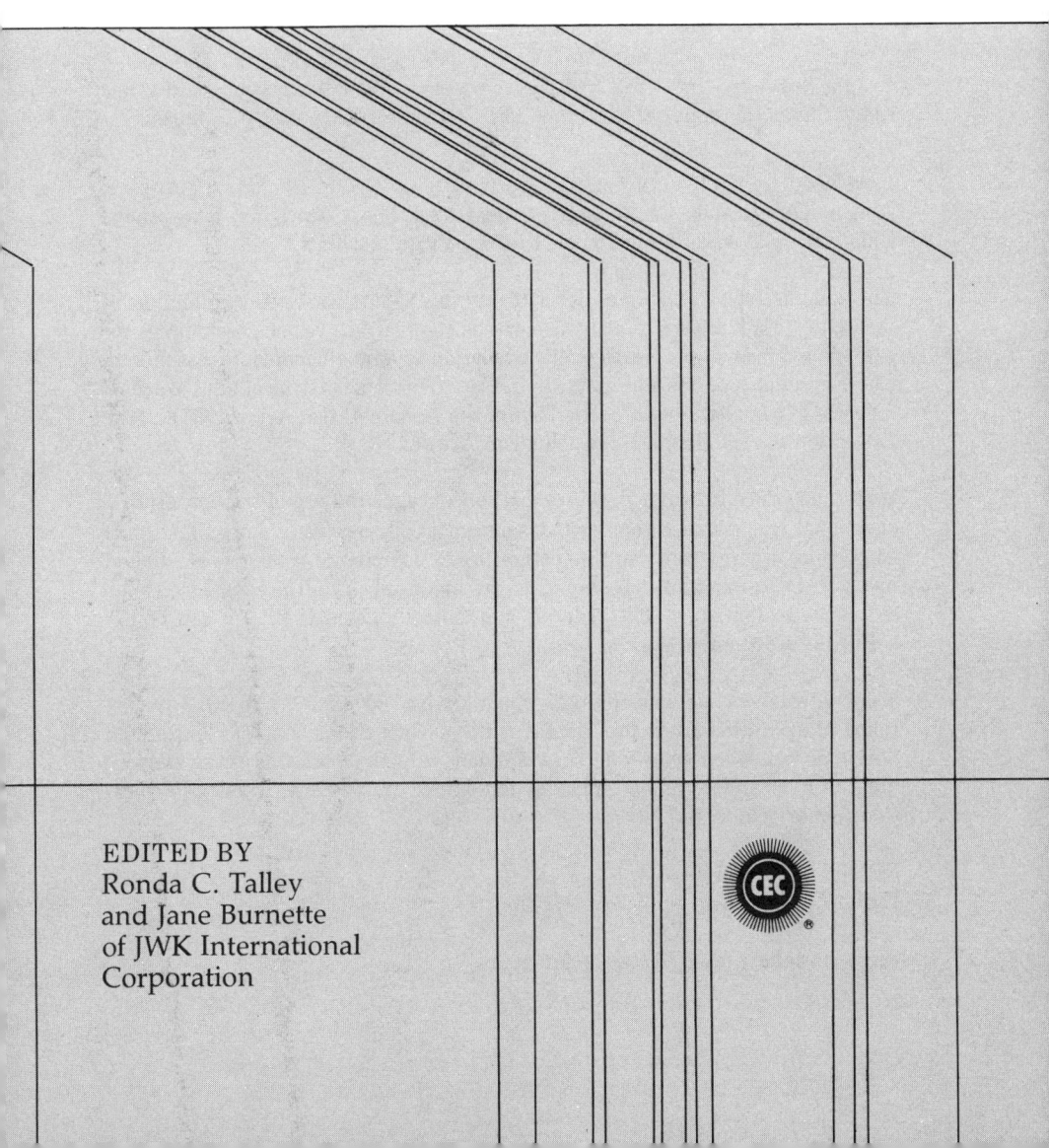

EDITED BY
Ronda C. Talley
and Jane Burnette
of JWK International
Corporation

© Linc Services, Inc. 1982. All rights reserved. For permissions and other rights under this copyright, contact The Council for Exceptional Children.

Developed by JWK International Corporation, 7617 Little River Turnpike, Annandale, Virginia 22003, and published by The Council for Exceptional Children, 1920 Association Drive, Reston, Virginia 22091.

The administrative strategies described in this report were selected and documented by JWK International Corporation to illustrate various techniques for providing a free, appropriate public education to mildly handicapped students. The document contains administrative strategies which may be helpful to school districts in complying with Section 504 of the Rehabilitation Act of 1973 and the Education for All Handicapped Children Act of 1975.

While the Office for Civil Rights (OCR) encourages the use of this material, it should not be construed that such use automatically assures a determination of compliance when a complaint investigation or compliance review is conducted by OCR. Determinations of compliance are made only after the completion of an extensive examination that includes much more information than can be described in a document such as this.

This material was developed under Contract No. 300-79-062 to JWK International Corporation from the Department of Education. Opinions expressed herein do not necessarily reflect the opinions or policy positions of the Department of Education, and no official endorsement by the Department of Education should be inferred.

ISBN 0-86586-126-9
Library of Congress Number 81-71936

Printed in the United States of America

Contents

Introduction: The Administrative Challenge, *Ronda C. Talley* 1

1. Administrative Systems for Service Delivery, *Thomas E. Oliver* 5
   Streamlining the referral to placement process. Managing an increased workload. Planning. Acquiring and allocating resources.

2. Community Involvement, *George W. Shellem* 39
   A categorization of supplemental resources. Utilization of community resources. Interagency agreements. Contractual arrangements for utilizing community resources.

3. Communication, *Sharon L. Raimondi* 65
   The external public. The internal public.

4. Personnel Utilization, *Ronda C. Talley* 83
   Creating or redefining personnel roles. Strategies for using teams and paraprofessionals.

5. Staff Development, *Susan E. Elting* 112
   Planning staff development programs. Job-embedded staff development. Job-related staff development.

6. Conclusion, *Ronda C. Talley* 146

Appendix: Identification of Problem Areas, Sites, and Administrative Strategies, *Ronda C. Talley* 148

Special Education in Transition

A Series Publication of
The Council for Exceptional Children

June B. Jordan, Editor in Chief
Gale S. Adams, Managing Editor

Series Editor: Maynard C. Reynolds

Consulting Editors:

Jack I. Bardon, University of North Carolina at Greensboro
Alejandro Benavides, Chicago Board of Education
Diane Bricker, University of Oregon
Dean C. Corrigan, University of Maryland
Julia Davis, University of Iowa
Stanley L. Deno, University of Minnesota
Jerry C. Gross, New York City Public Schools
John Guthrie, International Reading Association

Reginald L. Jones, University of California, Berkeley
Barbara K. Keogh, University of California at Los Angeles
Garry McDaniels, Bureau of Education for the Handicapped
Joseph S. Renzulli, University of Connecticut
Rosemary C. Sarri, University of Michigan
Judy A. Schrag, Washington State Department of Public Instruction
Donald J. Stedman, The University of North Carolina

Introduction:

The Administrative Challenge

RONDA C. TALLEY

Administrators in our nation's schools are facing greater challenges than ever before as they work to provide all students with a free, appropriate public education in the least restrictive environment. Educators are now successfully addressing a host of issues surrounding the provision of appropriate services to students. These issues are diverse, but they have been met with determination and innovation by state and local education agency (SEA and LEA) administrators throughout the country.

National awareness of the need to integrate handicapped students and to provide them with individually determined, appropriate services has grown over the past two decades. Educational administrators in many states have grappled with the complex issues involved in moving handicapped students from segregated classes and facilities and preparing their public educational systems to receive and appropriately serve these students. Two pieces of federal legislation, the Rehabilitation Act of 1973 and the Education for All Handicapped Children Act of 1975, acknowledged this trend toward individualized education for all handicapped students and emphasized the need for national attention to these issues. Additionally, Section 504 of the Rehabilitation Act of 1973 requires that federal funds cannot be supplied to any agency which discriminates on the basis of handicapping condition.

According to the Public Law 94-142 regulations, a free appropriate public education (a) is provided at public expense, under public supervision and direction, and without charge; (b) meets the standards of the state education agency; (c) includes preschool, elementary, and secondary school education in the state involved; and (d) is provided in conformity with an individualized education program (34 CFR §300a. 4).

Thus, the appropriate educational setting for a student is defined by that student's individualized educational program, and is determined on the basis of two criteria: maximal integration into the regular class and maximal contact with nonhandicapped peers.

As administrators began implementing these mandates, it became apparent that there was a need for additional information on how to address the complex issues involved. Moving students to less restrictive environments and providing a full range of services generally affects all levels of school administration. Past research has indicated that although problems may occur at all levels, solutions to many of them—even some classroom or building level problems—are often more effectively dealt with at a broad administrative level. Many solutions require resources that are controlled at the state or local administrative level and some problems must be attended to on a district-wide basis. In addition, SEA and LEA administrators can greatly affect the climate for action at the teacher-student level.

To meet the administrator's need for information, the Office of Special Education (OSE) and the Office for Civil Rights (OCR) funded several technical assistance projects. One of these was a project performed by JWK International Corporation to identify critical problems and to document successful, field-based, administrative strategies. This handbook, aimed at local education agency administrators, is a product of that project.

IDENTIFYING PROBLEM AREAS AND DOCUMENTING ADMINISTRATIVE STRATEGIES

Administrative strategies are defined as those techniques which facilitate the successful provision to handicapped students of appropriate education in least restrictive environments. These methods are used at the system level and focus on the school system as an organizational entity. They are distinct from those used at the classroom level, which focus on individual teacher-student interactions. These strategies, while initially conceptualized and integrated into LEA policy by administrators, may be delegated to a variety of administrative, supportive, and instructional staff members for actual implementation.

The strategies described in this handbook were identified through a two-stage nomination process. First, five states were selected on the basis of nominations from persons with a national perspective of special education, including representatives of national educational organizations, the Office of Special Education, regional resource centers operated under OSE funding, state special education directors, and numerous university personnel. Within these states 30 local education agencies which had developed innovative techniques were identified. Visits to each agency and interviews with numerous persons involved in the operation of each strategy verified that the strategies were considered successful and provided the descriptive information presented in this handbook. The Appendix provides a detailed description of the method used to identify problem areas in the integration of handicapped students, the procedure used to identify and document strategies which address these problems, and a brief summary of the special education service delivery system used by each of the five states and 30 local education agencies which contributed strategies to this study.

Although many sound techniques were observed in the districts that were included in this study, the reader should not assume that this handbook provides evidence for the legal compliance of these districts with Public Law 94-142 or Section 504. While the Office of Special Education and the Office for Civil Rights encourage use of the strategies described in this volume, it should not be construed that such use automatically assures a determination of compliance when a complaint investigation or compliance review is conducted by OSE or OCR. Determinations of compliance are made only after the completion of an extensive examination that includes much more information than can be described in a volume such as this.

Initially, it was expected that the problem areas for integrating mildly handicapped students and the strategies which addressed these areas would differ from those relating to students with severe handicaps; thus, the project was divided into two components. Upon investigation, however, many of the field-based strategies used with severely handicapped students were found to be the same as those used with mildly handicapped students. (Later project activities dropped the distinction between these sets of administrative strategies and dealt with all handicapped students.) This handbook describes more than 100 administrative strategies identified by the portion of the project which dealt with the integration of mildly handicapped students; some of the strategies presented may also be effective in integrating severely handicapped students.

For the purpose of this project, mildly handicapped was defined not by type of handicap, but by degree of disability. Mildly handicapped students are those persons considered handicapped under Public Law 94-142 or Section 504 but who are served for part or all of the school day in regular education classes. Thus, this definition depends on providing the appropriate setting for the student.

This handbook is directed toward school administrators in the belief that *administrators are the key persons in implementing change* within a school district. In addition to being in a leadership role, administrators typically possess the authority and control the funds needed to implement change. Furthermore, they are able to obtain a system level perspective that can enable them to judge a school district's needs, the techniques most likely to work within that district, and the potential for interaction (positive or negative) among those techniques. This handbook, which suggests methods for successfully implementing educational change, is therefore directed toward the local education agency administrator; however, the information on innovative strategies it contains may also be of interest to other school personnel and community members.

The provision of a free, appropriate public education within the least restrictive environment involves many complex issues. In addressing these issues, educational administrators may wish to use several or many of the strategies presented here, and should be concerned with the interaction of these strategies with other techniques and strategies in use or planned for use within their districts.

ORGANIZATION OF THIS HANDBOOK

Although the administrative strategies presented are organized according to five problem areas, *administrative systems for service delivery, community involvement, communication, personnel utilization, and staff development*, it is apparent that these five areas of administrative concern hardly form isolated issues. Success in implementing strategies that address one area of concern may be affected by the success of strategies in other areas. The interactive nature of problem areas and administrative strategies forms an important concept for the reader to keep in mind throughout this volume.

The handbook is organized into six chapters plus an appendix. Chapters 1 through 5 present information on strategies which address each of the five problem areas. The concluding section of each chapter is designed to stimulate thinking about which strategies are appropriate for use in the reader's district and ways the strategies might be adapted for local use. The Appendix offers information on the process used to identify and explore the problem areas and administrative strategies that were found in over 30 LEAs throughout five states.

The section concerning strategy selection is based on the assumption that three steps are needed to determine whether a strategy may be effectively used within an LEA. First, district administrators must conduct a study of the issues involved in providing a free, appropriate public education to handicapped students in least restrictive environments within their districts. This step ensures that district administrators are aware of the LEA's strengths and weaknesses in meeting state and federal mandates related to the education of handicapped students. It also assures that administrative staff are knowledgeable regarding these issues, and allows the relevant issues to be ranked in order of their importance in meeting district needs. Second, LEA administrators should determine the resources which are available to implement strategies. This step allows for the assessment of current resources and the identification of additional resources which may be essential in strategy implementation. Third, administrators, on the basis of available resources and district characteristics, should study strategy characteristics in order to select strategies which are best suited to their district's needs.

Local education agencies can provide each other with a wealth of information concerning effective methods for operationalizing the mandate to provide a free, appropriate public education to all students within the least restrictive environment. The basic purpose of this project was to assist in this sharing of information among LEAs by discussing with administrators their problems and innovative solutions in implementing this mandate and by validating, analyzing, and disseminating that information.

1

Administrative Systems for Service Delivery

THOMAS E. OLIVER

A significant outcome of recent federal legislation has been the expansion of the special education domain. The legislation has broadened the client base and the settings in which special education services are to be provided. Thus, more students are included in a special education domain that also includes an expanded number of services. In addition, the domain of special education is converging to a greater extent with regular education and now includes not only students and special education instructional staff, but also regular education staff and hosts of other professionals, parents, and advocates who were previously considered external to that domain.

Accordingly, special education administrative and delivery systems are expanding both in breadth and in complexity. Administrative systems are being restructured to provide school leaders with management procedures and service delivery systems modified in an effort to assure all students a free, appropriate public education in the least restrictive environment.

Expansion of the special education domain has presented numerous challenges to administrators concerned with efficient operation of the special education system. Administrators are responsible for directing change and for providing greater coordination among components of their educational systems. With an expanding scope of activities in the face of declining resources, their careful attention to planning is needed now more than ever before.

Many local education agencies (LEAs) have responded to these challenges in a rational manner, instituting systematic procedural and organizational changes which reflect the needs and demands of their educational systems. The changes which have been instituted mirror the diversity and range of challenges which LEAs are now called on to address.

This chapter discusses procedural and organizational changes that assist LEAs to better meet client needs. The first section includes strategies which streamline referral to placement systems in order to reduce overloads caused by an expanded client base and expanded services. The second section describes strategies which help manage increased workloads, including ways to promote efficient time utilization and to use computers to manage information for reporting purposes. The remaining sections provide models for planning and for acquiring and allocating resources.

In reviewing these strategies, it is essential for the reader to understand that while some strategies are directed specifically toward facilitating education in the least restrictive environment, other strategies facilitate integration indirectly. All strategies contained within this chapter are directed toward assisting administrators to provide a free, appropriate public education for handicapped students in our nation's schools.

STREAMLINING THE REFERRAL TO PLACEMENT PROCESS

The broadened special education client base has rendered traditional procedures for referring students for special services unwieldy. Local education agencies have been overwhelmed by the number of students and the volume of paperwork generated by traditional procedures. Two basic approaches to reducing this overload are presented in the following sections. These are prereferral services and streamlined referral and assessment procedures. The following strategies exemplify various administrative and organizational arrangements that have been used within each approach.

Utilizing Prereferral Services

Generally, prereferral services have two common goals: to reduce the number of students referred for formal evaluation and to assure that attempts have been made to educate the student in the regular classroom by modifying the program or classroom environment. In general, the prereferral process provides a regular classroom teacher with direct support from the principal, special education teachers, and/or other specialists in response to a student need or problem. This regular education process is not as formal or complex as procedures required for referral to special education. Its goal is to assist the student in meeting his or her educational objectives within the regular class. If the prereferral process is not successful in meeting this goal, the student is referred for formal evaluation and assessment.

These strategies have the additional benefit of providing regular education teachers with more information about classroom and program modifications that can assist students within the regular education classroom. In many cases, the prereferral process can help regular education teachers fill student needs in the classroom, avoiding the need for formal referral.

Team Approaches to Prereferral

Many LEAs have used teams to provide informal evaluations and consultation to classroom teachers. However, in various LEAs, teams perform different functions in addition to the two main functions previously described. They may also be organized differently or composed of persons in different professional roles. Most teams meet weekly and limit their discussions to a predetermined period of time or to a small number of cases. The following scenario describes a team meeting.

> At the beginning of the meeting, the referring teacher shares concerns about the child, and forms are used to record a description of what the teacher would like the child to be able to do in class, specific assets and deficits in the child's performance, and suggestions from the team. The group reviews each suggestion and indicates whether it is a possible or viable solution. The referring teacher is then asked whether each suggestion is acceptable. Suggestions deemed possible and acceptable are ranked according to priority and constitute a plan. Two follow-up meetings are held to review student progress and discuss suggestions which worked best.

The following discussions provide examples of how prereferral teams are used by four LEAs. Table 1 shows which professionals are included as team members in each of the LEAs.

Child study teams. Humbolt-Del Norte School District in California uses child study teams composed of special and regular educators. Teams vary in size, but generally have four to eight members. Most teams have more regular education teachers than special education teachers. Teams meet weekly and the meetings are limited to one hour. One team member observes the child in question and provides members with feedback on the team process.

Team members are selected by their principals after applying for membership on the team. The child study team application package contains a brief description of the team and how it works (adapted from the work of James C. Chalfant, Margaret VanDusen Pysh, and Robert Moultrie, 1979), a section outlining the responsibilities of the LEA and local school staff, and a list of steps for completing and submitting the application and implementation timelines. Members are released for a two-day training session which includes procedural information for making referrals, techniques for analyzing behavior, effective communication techniques, and procedures involved in implementing and conducting meetings. Team members receive a binder containing suggested techniques, referral forms, and examples of plans developed for students.

Referrals to the child study teams are made by individual teachers, who submit a form to the resource specialist. Additional information is then gathered from the child's teachers, cumulative files, or classroom observations.

School guidance committees. School guidance committees were created in Stanislaus, California, as an adaptation of the child study team model. They vary from the child study team model in their composition (see Table 1) and

TABLE 1
Comparison of Prereferral Team Personnel

Model	Principal	L.D. Teacher	Resource Teacher	Social Worker	School Nurse	Reading Specialist	Guidance Counselor	Psychologist	Speech/Language Clinician	Special Education Teacher	Regular Education Teacher	Title I Specialist	Community Agency Representative
Child Study Team	X									X	X		
School Guidance Committee					X		X			X	X		X
Building Screening Committees[a]	X		X	X	X	X	X		X	X	X		
Learning Team I–Elementary	X[b]	X	X	X	X	X	X	X	X	X	X		
Learning Team II–Elementary	X[b]	X	X	X	X	X	X	X	X	X		X	
Learning Team III–Secondary	X	X	X	X	X		X	X[b]					X

[a] Membership varies. Personnel noted are typically team members.
[b] Designates Learning Team chairperson.

training requirements. Whereas child study teams foster a greater regular education representation, guidance committees favor a representation of special educators. This modification to the strategy was made in order to minimize the differences between new procedures and the school system's established operating procedures. It was expected that school district personnel would more readily accept the modified strategy since it does not involve intensive training of classroom teachers.

Principals do not typically serve on the committee, but play a supporting role to the committee members. A sign-up sheet, located in the principal's office, is used to initiate the referral. Committee meetings are limited to discussions of three referrals. Minutes of each meeting are kept by the resource teacher and a copy is sent to the district office.

Building screening committees. A third approach to prereferral is to use a building screening committee, as is done in Shawnee Mission, Kansas. In this LEA, the initial referral is made by the teacher directly to the screening committee. The committee meets weekly to review problems and to make recommendations. Committee membership may vary, but represents a broad range of professionals, typically including the personnel indicated in Table 1.

Screening committees in the various school buildings generally follow similiar procedures, sharing pertinent information including performance and achievement levels, cumulative record information, classroom behavior, and known information regarding the home environment. Attempts at classroom modification recommended by the team may include providing direct services by specialists either in the regular classroom, in small groups outside of the classroom, or in a one-to-one setting outside the classroom.

Learning teams. At the present time, each building in the Arlington, Massachusetts, school district uses a learning team. While the purpose of the learning team is consistent across the LEA, the process by which teams function varies as a reflection of the educational setting and decisions of the building principals.

During the first few years of operation, records indicate that team members made efforts to define their roles and functions to meet the needs and demands of students in their schools. The district appears to have adopted three learning team variations, each composed of different members. Each of these three variations includes some mechanism for prereferral screening before a student's case is discussed by the learning team.

In the first elementary model shown in Table 1, a learning team chaired by the principal meets weekly. Referral is initiated when a parent, teacher, specialist, or principal completes a referral form. The referral is investigated by the principal. At this point, a decision to modify the regular classroom might be made, and if the modification is successful, it will, in effect, end the process. If not, the referral is scheduled for presentation to the learning team.

The second elementary model includes a coordinating team in addition to the learning team. The coordinating team meets biweekly, allowing team members time to meet with teachers, observe children in class, and conduct prereferral evaluations on alternate weeks. This informal interaction, as the initial step in the referral process, leads to investigation and discussion by the coordinating team and subsequent suggestions for classroom modification.

At the secondary school level, a referral team is used in addition to learning teams. The referral team meets weekly to screen students and to select members of a learning team for each individual student. Using this model, a number of three- or four-person learning teams function simultaneously, each assigned to a single student. Referral begins when the teacher completes a short form in the guidance office and discusses concerns with the student's counselor. If the teacher and counselor do not resolve the problem, the referral goes to the referral team. Within two weeks, the referral team selects a learning team to explore the problem. Then, a more intensive process is initiated. The learning team coordinates information, develops and implements a plan for the student, and reports back to the referral team within six weeks from the date the student's name initially appears on the agenda.

Implementing Team Approaches

Each of the models described was considered highly successful in reducing referrals at minimal cost. Data reported by five schools in Humboldt-Del Norte show that the number of formal referrals was reduced by the child study teams and that the local schools saved approximately 15 hours of specialists' time for each student who was not subsequently referred for formal evaluation. Arlington, Massachusetts, reports that the learning team process has resulted in a high rate (95%) of valid referrals.

In order to initiate a strategy such as this, it is essential that direction and support be provided by the building principal. Overall, primary concern should be given to setting up the team approach, planning for unique building needs, and staff scheduling.

Costs vary with training requirements, the number of professionals involved, and the amount of time required for team meetings and associated work. County staff of Humboldt-Del Norte reported that program expenditures for initial implementation of this strategy were minimal. Training involved the costs of one consultant, rental of a meeting room, and substitute teacher salaries for the two-day session. Implementation required the use of a half-time program specialist to provide feedback and further training as needed.

Although the teams described here perform the same basic functions, a number of variations are notable. In some districts, there is little variability among the personnel and procedures of teams operating in different schools. In other districts, considerable flexibility in determining the roles and functions of team personnel is considered an asset because it allows the team to adapt to the needs of the school and its students. In yet another district, an observer was assigned to provide members with feedback on the team process.

Service options also varied. While in most districts prereferral teams suggest modifications to the regular classroom or techniques to be used by the regular teacher, building screening committees had the additional option of providing a specialist in the regular class, in small groups, or in a one-to-one setting. Table 2 provides a comparison of several characteristics of prereferral team models.

In addition to reducing formal referrals and assuring that classroom modifications have been made, this strategy has several indirect benefits. Its use increases the awareness of regular teachers and other team members regarding classroom modifications and allows them to generally share their expertise. At the same time, the strategy assures more appropriate placement of students with discernible needs.

Prereferral Screening by Specialists

Some Massachusetts LEAs use generic teachers to assist with the establishment, coordination, reporting and monitoring of in-class modifications. A generic teacher is one who has received training in special education, with emphasis on a diagnostic/prescriptive approach to instructional programming. Generic teachers serve as the major source of communication between regular education and special education staff within a building.

When a regular education teacher feels that a student should be referred for evaluation, the generic or special education teacher is contacted. The two (or in some cases, more) teachers will meet to discuss the nature of the referral and possible program, environmental, or instructional modifications. A pre-evaluation conference will be held. Attendance may vary, but always includes the parent(s) and a selected member of the formal evaluation team appropriate to the nature of the reported problem (e.g., speech and language). The purpose of this meeting is to provide parents with the necessary information regarding the student's performance, corrective measures being considered, and information about parent and student rights under due process. The parent, at this time, may request a formal evaluation. Provided the parent agrees with the less formal course of action, the generic teacher will assist the regular education teacher in any of four ways: (a) by providing materials to the teacher; (b) by demonstrating methods and materials in the classroom; (c) by providing direct, short-term instruction to the student in the classroom; or (d) by observing student behavior in the classroom.

All program and classroom modification must be documented and available in the student's confidential file. Should these changes be unsuccessful, or should special education personnel desire a more formal evaluation, the regular education teacher must complete an individual referral form with the assistance of the generic teacher. The school principal is responsible, thereafter, for initiating the formal assessment process.

This strategy allows teachers to obtain assistance with classroom modifications, instructional techniques, and materials without the need for additional resources. The generic teacher is considered ideally suited for providing this assistance. Also, a separate and less complex pre-evaluation conference guarantees the rights of parents and students by providing them with information, obtaining their input, and facilitating the adaptation of the regular classroom to the student's needs prior to formal referral.

TABLE 2
Comparison of Prereferral Team Models

Prereferral Team Model	Person Receiving Referral from Classroom Teacher	Personnel	Possible Outcomes	Frequency of Meetings	Other Considerations
Child Study Team	• Resource Specialist	• Principal • Special and regular education teachers (Emphasis on regular education)	• modify classroom • refer to special education	• weekly (1 hour)	• 2-day training for team members • school based
School Guidance Committee	• Principal	• Counselors • Regular teachers • Special teachers • School nurse	• modify classroom • refer to special education	• determined by school	• school based
Building Screening Committee	• Screening Committee	• Varies with case	• modify classroom • provide specialists in classroom, in small groups, or one-to-one	• weekly	• school based
Learning Team	• Principal	• Principal • LD teacher • Resource teacher • School nurse • Counselor • Others (varies with model)	• modify classroom after investigation by principal, coordinating team, or referral team • refer to formal evaluation by full learning team	• weekly	• school based

Implementation

Difficulties encountered when this process was first implemented were: (a) classroom teachers' resistance to changing their classroom behavior, (b) teachers' reluctance to seek and accept assistance from the generic teacher, and (c) reluctance to complete required documentation forms. These difficulties were reportedly resolved as a result of the principal's involvement in and endorsement of the pre-evaluation process.

In one LEA, 1,150 referrals had been made in the year prior to the establishment of the pre-evaluation process. Of this total, 65-70% (about 775) were considered appropriate and valid. Following the implementation of the strategy, 750 referrals were made, of which 95% (about 712) were considered appropriate.

Summary: Prereferral Services

It is interesting to note that when resolving the problems associated with student referrals, local education agencies have identified and manipulated a common element, the number of student referrals. It is also of interest that a number of states used team strategies, including Massachusetts, a state that also uses individuals to perform prereferral screening.

Certainly of value is the child study team, presented here as a unique approach directed toward reducing student referrals for comprehensive evaluation and providing prereferral classroom intervention. The benefits derived from this model are far-reaching, especially since this model fosters regular educators' involvement. Classroom teachers take an active role in this process, solving problems in ways formerly thought privy to special educators.

Other strategies also resulted in positive outcomes. For example, through the pre-evaluation process, beneficial contacts between generic teachers and classroom teachers are made. The assistance provided to the classroom teachers is almost always available by nature of the generic teacher's role—it is the generic teacher's full-time responsibility to consult with teachers and other specialists.

The models presented here use common elements. The variations have occurred not haphazardly, but have developed over a period of time in accordance with the individual LEA's needs, established protocol, and historical structure. One of the major concerns of these LEAs was to plan and implement changes which proved least threatening to the established way of doing things.

STREAMLINING ASSESSMENT AND EVALUATION PROCEDURES

The use of teams and individuals to streamline the referral to placement process does not exist solely at the prereferral level; other local education agencies have attempted to streamline the postreferral evaluation and assessment process. Corpus Christi, Texas, Little Falls, Minnesota, and Natick, Massachusetts, have implemented strategies to streamline the evaluation and assessment process.

Appraisal Teams

In the Corpus Christi Independent School District, the concept of using teams of specialists to collect and interpret assessment information appears more efficient than traditional approaches, and offers greater continuity in the delivery of diagnostic services. After a student is referred for evaluation, an Admissions, Review, and Dismissal Committee develops a one page individualized educational plan (IEP) which suggests activities, goals, and materials to be used by the teachers. Then the appraisal team collects and interprets assessment data, and develops a detailed educational plan for the student.

Appraisal teams, comprised of an associate school psychologist and an educational diagnostician, are assigned to an area cluster. Each cluster includes a high school, two junior high schools, and five or six elementary schools. The appraisal team is scheduled to be at each school one day every other week. The teams, supported by special education funds, Public Law 94-142 funds, and local funds, are under the Director of Developmental Services and the Chief Psychologist, who provide direction, control, and supervision.

The two appraisal team members have different but complementary roles in the diagnostic process. The role of the associate school psychologist is to administer, score, and interpret psychological and educational tests, and to make recommendations for remediation. The psychologist also serves as a resource person to regular and special educators, administrators, and other professional staff; serves as a liaison with other community agencies concerned with physical and mental health, public welfare, and education; and may be involved in parent conferences.

The educational diagnostician assists with appraisals of learning and behavior problems, putting particular emphasis on identifying students' learning skills and recommending remediation techniques. The diagnostician also consults with professional staff, parents, and community agencies. The diagnostician's background in education and at least three years of teaching experience add credibility to the team, and his or her ability to translate the psychological assessment into educational plans aids the acceptance and implementation of instructional programs.

The appraisal team helps to ensure an orderly, systematic, and consistent system for delivering diagnostic services to handicapped children. The assignment of each team to a cluster of schools promotes the team's knowledge of the children's environment and subculture. Since the clusters include elementary, junior high, and high schools, teams have the opportunity to know the children for an extended length of time. In addition, they may develop long-term relationships with professionals working within the cluster and experience increased interaction with these professionals.

At the student level, appraisal teams have several additional benefits. First, high quality, accurate data on students are collected. Second, teachers receive almost immediate feedback and direction on instructional activities to meet the needs of students. This feedback takes the form of a one page IEP, developed by the members of the Admissions, Review, and Dismissal Committee. This initial IEP suggests activities, goals, and materials that a teacher can use until the more detailed educational plan is developed by the educational diagnostician. Third, the availability of ongoing support and consultative services facilitates cooperation and acceptance by regular educators. Fourth, the supervision of the appraisal team by one Chief Psychologist assures the continued quality of psychological assessments.

Diagnostic Teams

Diagnostic teams in Little Falls, Minnesota, are composed of two school psychologists and a social worker. One feature of this strategy that sets it apart from the appraisal team is the involvement of diagnostic team members in direct individual and/or group counseling with students who require such services. This service is important for a variety of reasons. Because of the involvement of the diagnostic team members in the assessment process, their counseling is more effective and less time is needed to establish a cooperative relationship with the student. Further, it is important for members of the team to be involved in the provision of direct service so that they maintain direct contact with the educational process.

The use of diagnostic teams has provided the district with higher quality evaluation and assessment data and has enhanced the development of a total picture of the strengths and weaknesses of each individual child. In addition, it has enhanced the timeliness of the referral and evaluation process.

Implementation of this strategy is similar but more complex than implementation of appraisal teams. Since psychologists and social workers perform counseling as well as assessment functions, more of their time is needed and scheduling to include the two types of activities may be more difficult.

Evaluation Team Chairpersons

Natick, Massachusetts, uses former generic teachers as evaluation team chairpersons who perform the following functions: (a) to expedite the fulfillment of due process requirements and state assessment and placement timelines and guidelines; (b) to monitor the development and implementation of IEPs; and (c) to assist in the appropriate placement of students who have completed their formal education, yet require further special services. However, generic teachers are not trained in assessment and evaluation as are psychologists and educational diagnosticians and they work within a somewhat different organizational arrangement.

Evaluation team chairpersons are housed within school buildings, where they serve both as monitors and as the local education agency representatives in formal evaluation procedures. They delegate tasks among evaluation team members and see that evaluation is timely and complete. They act as case managers, assuring that all responses to inquiries are handled by one person, and are responsible for the development and writing of the IEP. In addition, chairpersons are responsible for scheduling and completing paperwork for all reevaluation meetings.

The chairpersons have gradually been authorized to act on local school matters in the special education director's stead. The salaries of all team chairpersons are paid by the local education agency and additional funds are available to employ part-time generic teachers on an hourly basis to assist the chairpersons when their workloads prove too great. It has been reported that team chairpersons have virtually eliminated evaluation backlog and that of 1,050 (full, intermediate, and review) evaluations, only 10 required the special education director's intervention. Thus, the major outcome of this strategy is the refinement and expedition of the evaluation process.

Comparison of Postreferral Evaluation and Assessment Strategies

The three strategies discussed in this section represent methods of implementing the IEP process that is required by law. Each strategy has unique characteristics that may be seen as particularly beneficial to one of the persons involved. Appraisal teams produce a detailed educational plan on the basis of the IEP, benefiting the teacher. Diagnostic teams provide direct counseling to students, which may relieve some of the workload of school counselors. Finally, evaluation team chairpersons perform an administrative function, monitoring and coordinating the evaluation to placement process and acting as case managers.

Each of these strategies has other unique advantages as well. Appraisal teams provide personal consultation and support to teachers, administrators, and other professionals through the school psychologist. The teams additionally provide prompt response to teachers' requests for assistance, followed by a more detailed response later. Diagnostic teams provide counseling to students and create a closer relationship between the student's educational and counseling environments. Evaluation team chairpersons provide overall coordination of the student's case. Although each strategy has unique characteristics which may make it more appropriate for the needs of a particular school district, the overall result produced by the strategies is the same—to expedite the formal evaluation and assessment process.

Summary: Evaluation and Assessment Procedures

It is perhaps difficult to appreciate that any process, including the referral to placement process, can be streamlined by creating additional organizational units. After all, the natural tendency of additional units is to institute their own operating procedures, which increases organizational complexity. However, several characteristics of these pre- and postreferral strategies counter this tendency. The prereferral strategies substitute a less complex operation for the more formal and complex evaluation and assessment procedure. All of the strategies emphasize the assignment of specific duties and responsibilities to teams or individuals. These duties often are designed to relieve an overload of work for persons in other, more traditional roles. In addition, and perhaps most importantly, each of the strategies was designed to increase communication and coordination among other units within the educational system. Increased coordination and communication are essential to the integration of handicapped students, since providing such an education calls for greater interaction of the regular and special education systems. In addition, increased coordination of educational system components can help to provide an expanded scope of services with more efficient use of resources.

MANAGING AN INCREASED WORKLOAD

LEA administrators must now devote more time to planning, budgeting, and meeting state and federal information requirements than ever before, leaving them less time to plan and monitor daily activities in the schools.

Given the numbers of students served by local education agencies and the large amount of paperwork, conferences, and planning involved in integrating handicapped students, it is not surprising that teachers and administrators alike rate time as one of the resources on which the greatest demands are made. Lack of time is also thought to be one problem about which little can be done. This section addresses strategies designed to promote efficient utilization of time through the use of time management studies and workshops and innovative uses of computer systems.

Improving Utilization of Time

Teachers as well as administrators are being subjected to increased demands on their time. Efficient use of time has become more and more important. As the amount of time teachers spend on required paperwork and other noninstructional activity increases, time spent in direct service to students may decrease. The first strategy discussed in this section is the time utilization study, which investigates how the teacher's workday is actually spent, showing which activities are actually receiving highest priority in terms of time usage. Results may then be compared to desirable priorities, allowing more control over real time usage so that it may better reflect desirable time allocation.

The second strategy presented is the time management workshop, a form of in-service training in techniques to minimize inefficiency and gain better control of how time is spent. A workshop for teachers was held in the Humbolt-Del Norte School District, California, and one for principals was held in Comal, Texas.

Time Utilization Study

The purpose of the time-motion study was to assess the length and percentage of time teachers spent providing services to handicapped students and related activities during a one week period in Humbolt-Del Norte, California. Teachers volunteered to participate in this study. The LEA attempted to obtain a relatively uniform sample regarding the grade levels taught, the type of resource teacher (i.e., school based or itinerant), and the size of the schools in which the resource teachers provided special services.

Formal approval was needed to allocate special education funds in order to implement this study. It was necessary to hire and train 10 data collectors, reimburse school districts for substitute teachers in order to release the 20 teachers for training (half-day), hire a clerk to tabulate data and prepare it for dissemination, and reimburse data collectors and resource teachers for travel expenses (i.e., mileage).

After selection and categorization of activities to be observed, forms for data collection were developed and field tested. Then 10 data collectors were selected and trained by LEA quasiadministrative personnel in the use of the forms.

Each resource teacher was observed by a data collector from 8:00 a.m. to 4:00 p.m. for five working days. Time spent in each of the designated activities was recorded and tabulated. The resource teachers were asked to submit estimates of the time spent in these activities prior to 8:00 a.m., after 4:00 p.m., and during the weekend (the study defined the work week as being Sunday to Sunday).

The study indicated that 35% of resource teachers' time was spent in direct instruction, 12% was used for indirect services (including required paperwork), 37% was used for coordinating services, and the remaining 16% was used for other related and nonrelated activities. The average length of the work week was 47 hours.

The total staff of 65 resource teachers was provided the results of this study and asked to estimate their own time spent in each of the activities under observation. This, in essence, provided the opportunity for self-evaluation. This information was used to develop a more complete profile of the resource teacher staff, and to develop an in-service package on better use of personal and professional time.

Various special education administrators and resource teachers reported genuine surprise that not as much time was being spent completing paperwork as most had thought. Another surprise was how little time was spent providing direct service to students.

Having been made aware of this information, resource teachers reported that they have been able to use their time in a more expedient manner and have endeavored to increase the time spent in providing direct service to children. The special education director felt that the information obtained through the study would be invaluable when planning systematic changes, projecting future needs, and discussing personal and professional concerns with resource teachers.

Time Management Workshops for Teachers

In response to the time utilization study, Humbolt-Del Norte conducted a workshop to promote more effective and efficient use of time. The four-hour workshop was offered to special education teachers and was chaired by a local college instructor who was considered an expert in the area of time management. Specific discussion concerned the use of time when communicating with people, excessive time involved in searching for materials, and scheduling.

When communicating with people, special education teachers are now better able to focus on topics, monitor conversations, and keep themselves and other persons focused on the topic under discussion. The teachers also find that this assists them in most conferences. They are now taking a more active role and are able to participate more.

Most special education teachers have now taken time to arrange their materials so that they can be quickly located. They are using notebooks to compile student information, notecards and file boxes to maintain accurate data on each child's progress on a task or within a curriculum, and separate sheets to plan daily activities and record weekly activities. These sheets are used as checklists for planning efficient time usage and staying on task. On both forms, teachers indicate the priority of each activity and whether its completion is an attainable goal for the day or week.

Overall, it seems that teachers have been pleased with the results of the time utilization workshop. They now have more time to provide direct service to handicapped students, and report that the workshop has produced greater awareness of personal and professional use of time and has relieved some of the frustrations of coping with daily activities. The success of the workshop for special education teachers led the district to provide a modified workshop for regular education teachers to promote the same time improvement activities.

Time Management Workshop for Administrators

Comal Independent School District conducted a less formal time management training activity which was directed toward administrators rather than teachers.

Based on his own experiences with time management seminars, the superintendent developed "leadership training activities" for district administrators. Administrators were asked to focus on current use of time and assess how much time they spent performing supervisory and administrative functions. They also analyzed the nature of the tasks performed in each category (administrative and supervisory) as well as "personal time wasters." They were asked to categorize tasks in terms of importance, thinking about those which could be delegated to others and those which could not. Finally, the training session participants discussed various methods and techniques that could be used to promote effective time management.

Several principals reported increased awareness of their use of time and a tendency to analyze the tasks they were doing or planning in a more systematic way. Another principal used time management techniques to structure special education referral meetings and found the process more productive when people had clearer expectations about the process and were aware of limitations or time constraints.

Summary: Improving Time Utilization

The strategies of this section provide administrative and instructional personnel not only with direct feedback on their use of time, but also with organizational tools to increase their efficiency. The time utilization study serves in a sense as a needs assessment—activities in which time could be better used are highlighted, and low priority activities that receive an inordinate amount of time are revealed.

The teachers' workshops developed on the basis of this information focused attention on setting priorities and realistic goals, developing organizational techniques, and using communications skills that reduce wasted time. The workshop for principals, in addition to providing information in these areas, placed emphasis on planning, task analysis, and task delegation. With today's increasing workloads, attention to organizational skills and efficiency can produce benefits that result in greater personal control of time, smoother organizational operations, and more time to devote to providing direct instruction to children.

Using Computers to Help Meet Information Requirements

Information demands made on LEAs are increasing in both amount and complexity. More complex budget preparation procedures are involved in meeting state and federal requirements. Statistical requirements are greater. And, as more students are mainstreamed and receive multiple services, the separation and estimation of costs for their education and related planning and reporting becomes more difficult.

Thus, special education administrators must devote more of their time to developing long-range, comprehensive plans (upon which budget approval depends), reporting information to other agencies, and maintaining accurate fiscal records. Local education agencies have by necessity developed various systems for collecting pertinent information, analyzing it, and making it readily accessible not only for reporting purposes, but also for planning and daily program operation. Those LEAs that have access to computers have found them invaluable in meeting these requirements.

The first two strategies discussed in this section describe how existing LEA computer systems have been modified to include special education subsystems. The final strategy of the section relates how an LEA contracted for computerized special education information management.

Using Existing Computer Systems to Maintain Data on Handicapped Students

The school districts discussed in this section have used computerized information systems to standardize and expedite the gathering and reporting of student and school information for the following purposes: to meet reporting requirements; to provide administrators with information necessary to plan for meeting future needs; to provide administrators, supervisors, and instructional personnel with information necessary for the operation of buildings and programs; and to a lesser degree, to investigate the effectiveness of special education practices and programs.

Dallas, Texas

Of the management information systems to be discussed in this section, the one used in Dallas, Texas, is the most extensive in that it produces the largest amount of information and provides this information to the greatest number of district employees. The Dallas information management system produces faculty and student rosters (by school and by classroom), letters to parents, mailing lists and labels, state surveys, civil rights surveys, state required statistical tabulations, statistical information for program and budget planning, information needed to obtain state and federal funding and other miscellaneous analyses (e.g., incidence tables of handicapping conditions in student enrollment). Of major importance is a child tracking system, in its pilot stage, which provides managers, administrators, and principals with a report of all special education services received by any one student.

Principals can obtain most information available to management, provided it is pertinent to students, schedules, or materials. In addition to routine information needs, principals can obtain health information, annual attendance projections, suspension records, lists of special education placements, individual due process records, bus schedules, special services schedules, free lunch program rosters, and ESEA program rosters.

At least six months were needed to create the data base and to provide for data analysis and retrieval. In developing the original data base, speech pathologists and prescriptive teachers gathered and encoded student data. This data consisted primarily of demographic information pertinent to routine special education management. The data were included in the master data base which contains information about all students.

Present data entry procedures include the assignment of an admission, review, and dismissal (ARD) team leader for each school to be responsible for entering new information and to see that the information is encoded, keypunched, and entered into the data base. This information is encoded by data technicians and the ARD team leader, keypunched by technicians, and delivered to the data processing division. The data processing division has provided a primary statistician and a number of assistants for executing requests.

Data technicians are assigned to most of the elementary schools, while at the secondary level, technicians travel among schools and gather information biweekly. Data technician positions are funded with state and federal monies augmented by local funds; in most cases, these are not special education funds.

Although users considered the system to be responsive, two difficulties were encountered: there were sometimes delays in obtaining responses to information requests, and sometimes the information supplied was not up to date. These problems were especially prone to occur during peak usage periods.

In order to alleviate these problems and to reduce overload at the principal statistician's office where information requests are received, a pilot project was undertaken to allow principals, managers, and other administrators to obtain data directly from the computer. Satellite communications terminals were installed at two schools and in-service training in their use was provided. It was thought that allowing users to request information directly could avoid overloads in processing requests and delays in entering new data, which result in the data base not being current. If this pilot project is successful, the LEA expects to expand the system in future years.

Contra Costa, California

The Management Information System (MIS) in Contra Costa, California, is a set of computer programs designed to provide reports needed to describe and analyze specific current operations. The system, which was implemented four years ago, was designed to allow the LEA to generate state and federal reports with a minimum of maintenance and to provide information to other special and regular education personnel.

Principals automatically receive quarterly reports that include the amount of money spent each quarter, rosters of special education students by campus, teacher case loads, case load variation, and comparisons of revenue and needs. Teachers receive a quarterly listing of students and their total number of unexcused absences. Other information is available to teachers through their principals or through the MIS system directly. In addition, the teacher organization receives budget information in order to pursue its activities.

Planning the design of the system included the following activities: identifying the types of computer hardware available, investigating time-sharing options, conducting a needs assessment regarding the types of information required, developing time lines for collecting data, and developing a process for reporting information. Also important to the planning of the MIS system was the development of data collection forms. A staff member suggested that in order to avoid negative attitudes, the fact that the system includes a computer should not be emphasized; the computer should be incidental to the user, and forms should be completed by hand and should remain uncomplicated.

A tremendous amount of in-service training was involved in the implementation of this strategy. Training was originally directed to resource and program specialists who would, in turn, train other special education teachers. However, the principal planner reported that this limited staff training was not effective. In-service directly targeted toward teachers and aides was necessary. In-service continued for two years on a bimonthly basis, but it was also provided on demand and when the staff changed. The goals of in-service training were to promote acceptance of the MIS system, to explain the completion of forms, to explain how forms travel through the system, and to stress accuracy and timeliness in completing forms. A manual was developed to assist teachers in completing forms.

The cost of the MIS system includes the salaries of three coders and one data manager. This LEA owns its own computer and terminals. The cost of operating the computer is absorbed through a tax levy.

Contracting for Special Education Information Management

The LEA in Arlington, Massachusetts, obtains special education information management services by contract with a private firm because the LEA computers are already fully used. Information is gleaned from students' evaluation meeting reports, IEPs, and annual reviews. A member of the central administrative staff transfers the information from manual forms to data processing cards. The information recorded includes classification by level of service and classroom environmental restriction, category and hours of services recommended and provided, and the amount of time spent evaluating the student. Since the number of scheduled service hours and the actual amount of service provided are recorded, the administrator has an effective vehicle for monitoring services provided.

The programs are written in a way that allows information concerning the total special education student population to be organized by school, level of service restriction category, handicapping condition, and alphabetical order. Computer printouts indicating what special services have been provided in each school are distributed to principals every other month.

The system has provided the director of pupil personnel with monthly updates in an effective and efficient manner regarding the number of children receiving special education services, thus making reporting to the Massachusetts Department of Education a less difficult task. Staff time and energy have been used more efficiently, and collecting information for entry into the computer system has not increased the amount of paperwork done by special education teachers and specialists.

Summary: Using Computers

This section described three systems used by three very different local education agencies. Many local education agencies have contemplated the inclusion of computer services in their budget proposals, and as computer technology becomes more available at more reasonable costs, the ideas presented here may prove increasingly valuable.

Various computer systems have different capabilities for generating information. But, depending on the ways the systems are designed and used, local education agencies can benefit from automated information management systems when analyzing program effectiveness, efficiency, outcomes, and impact, and when planning for organizational change.

Summary: Managing an Increased Workload

The topics described in this section are examples of approaches that have been taken by LEA administrators in their efforts to cope with the complex processes and broadened scope of activities they must deal with today. Principals and teachers, in turn, must make the best use of their time, since they, too, are subjected to the pressures of an increased workload. By providing assistance in this area, the LEA can help to assure the most efficient use of employees' time.

Finally, special education information requirements have also increased dramatically, and the use of computers to save time, provide needed information for planning, and assess program efficiency has been found valuable by a number of LEAs.

PLANNING

Effective planning requires two elements: appropriate information, including the input of personnel representing a broad range of opinions, and time to adequately analyze, define, and outline each task. Thus, in order to plan for future needs and to assess the outcomes and impacts of programs in operation, one must have pertinent information from a broad range of sources.

Due to the inflexibility of their schedules, it is difficult to involve school faculty, supervisors, and administrators in planning for future activities. Planning has, therefore, often been performed primarily by administrators. This can be problematic when the desired change affects the regular education environment. The strategies reported here attempt to ensure that both appropriate personnel and adequate time are devoted to planning for organizational change.

Participatory Planning

Alternate methods of encouraging participation in the planning of learning centers (described in Chapter 4) in Shawnee Mission, Kansas, were investigated, and it was decided to subsidize the expenses of key personnel attending a specially designed university course. This course provided adequate information about the concepts and theories of learning centers and skills associated with designing and executing needs assessments, and also provided time for developing a plan for establishing learning centers at the building level.

Participants earned college credit for taking this course, which was directed and coordinated by the LEA's special education director. The course met one night per week for one semester. As a final product, the participants developed a plan for establishing learning centers, including system-wide planning and planning for centers within individual buildings.

Thus, the plan is the result of efforts made by individuals who represented various school positions and it takes into account their concerns and the demands placed on the allocation of resources. Due to the support and incentives offered by the LEA (i.e., tuition payment for college credit), the participants were highly motivated to devote their time and effort to the project, and, in addition, expressed a feeling of personal ownership of the plan. The opportunity for ongoing evaluation and revision, provided through the instructor's guidance and the personal commitment of the participants, appeared to contribute to the quality of the final plan.

The strategy is applicable in many subject areas appropriate for academic presentation. It requires making arrangements with a college or university that is either within reasonable traveling distance from the LEA or is willing to offer the course at a location accessible to LEA staff. LEA administrators need to work with the university to plan and develop the course, considering both LEA planning needs and academic requirements. Finally, the LEA needs resources to cover the costs of participants' attendance.

School Subcommittees

The original intent of the strategy was to establish a mechanism to facilitate budget oversight of district programs after a program budgeting system had been adopted. Prior to the establishment of subcommittees, presenting program needs to the full school committee (school board) was usually the responsibility of a single administrator. Thus, a program's budget depended largely on the success of a single individual in providing essential information to the committee.

Two years ago, the Arlington, Massachusetts, school committee established four subcommittees, one in each of the following areas: elementary education, secondary education, pupil personnel services, and maintenance and facilities. Three committee members serve on each subcommittee.

The full school committee meets every other week, and subcommittees meet alternate weeks. Typically, supervisors, principals, other educational staff members, and community members present information pertinent to budget, planning, and programming decisions. In addition, committee and subcommittee members who want more information or firsthand observation may elect to visit school programs.

During the first year of operation, the school committee chairman and the superintendent worked together to develop the subcommittee process. The chairman and another committee member selected subcommittee members. Some were permanently assigned to a single subcommittee while others were assigned to subcommittees according to an annually rotating schedule. Assistant superintendents appropriate to each area of concern were assigned to work with subcommittees, contributing their knowledge of specific programs and issues.

A primary outcome of the subcommittee process is that the school committee is better prepared and has more information for planning activities. As a result of the process, the time and energy of each committee member is devoted to one program area, rather than being diffused. It is reported that this process is cost and time efficient in that it is no longer necessary for all nine members of the full school committee to review each program or analyze each line of each budget proposal.

This strategy is a relatively simple organizational change that requires no additional resources or staff positions. It does, however, require additional time and effort on the part of the school committee chairman and superintendent for planning, and on the part of the assistant superintendent and all committee members who implement the strategy.

Special Education Planning Survey

San Juan Unified School District, California, with an average daily attendance of more than 55,000, was divided into two service delivery areas. Each of these areas is administered by a program supervisor and staffed by five area resource teachers who are assigned to approximately 10 schools, providing a variety of supportive services. In order to assess school administrators' satisfaction with current area office services and to gather information for planning, building principals were surveyed by special education program supervisors.

The Special Education Planning Survey was developed by the Research and Evaluation Department as a planning tool that would allow regular and special education administrators to review and discuss programs and services, identify problems, and plan for corrections or modifications. The instrument addressed various services and functions of office personnel, emphasizing 16 types of services offered by the area offices. Respondents were asked to indicate whether delivery of each service was adequate, inadequate, or not needed during the present year. Respondents were then asked to list major accomplishments and major problems experienced throughout the year. Principals' views regarding quantity of paperwork and other demands upon time, such as evaluation and assessment meetings, were solicited.

The survey was sent to every principal in the district. After allowing time for principals to develop their answers, the program supervisors from each area office scheduled interviews with 78% of the district's principals. Each interview required 30 to 60 minutes. Through the surveys and interviews, the principals identified major accomplishments and problems related to special education in their schools. The most frequently identified accomplishments were the successful integration and acceptance of handicapped students by the classroom teachers, successful identification and appropriate placement of students in special education programs, and successful programs provided to students by qualified and competent special education staff. Problems stated frequently by principals were the lack of communication and effective decision making at the school and area office level, lack of willingness by regular education program staff to work with special education students, and inadequate space, materials, and equipment.

Thus, the survey served as a planning tool to assess the impact of organizational change on special education and allowed the district to plan for further changes and modifications in programs. In addition, the meetings with principals provided a source of two-way communication. Various changes within individual schools were considered to result from the survey. For example, the review led to the establishment of the position of Special Education Department Chairperson at one high school, and a screening team process was set up at another school.

Program Implementation Review

Humbolt-Del Norte, California, with the assistance of a local higher education institution, also developed a planning survey. The success of this survey resulted in a permanent planning process called Program Implementation Review (PIR). Initially, the intent of the PIR was to monitor district compliance with the California Master Plan and the initial survey was funded under the Master Plan. Presently, it is an ongoing process of informal program analysis and evaluation. Humbolt and Del Norte counties began implementation of the Master Plan on a pilot basis in 1975–1976. During that year, major changes in organization and service delivery were made. In November, 1975, the county superintendent initiated a series of structured interviews to obtain input for possible Master Plan revision. Consultants from the local college designed and implemented the study which was followed by a report to the schools and a two-day conference which allowed people to air their views and solve problems. The conference was so successful that the director of special education decided to provide school staff with a forum in which they could continue making their needs and demands known. The result was the PIR, developed and implemented in 1976.

The assistant director of special education, program specialists, and district representatives participated in developing instrumentation and data collection procedures for the PIR. The 82-item instrument has four major sections: (a) general, (b) administrative, (c) resource specialist/special class, and (d) designated instruction and services.

Program specialists collected the data. Forms were sent to schools in the early spring, asking principals and teachers to complete appropriate sections individually. Then a program specialist visited each school, meeting with staff to develop a composite review for each school. Data gathering took 2-3 weeks and averaged 2 hours per school. County office staff compiled the individual school reports and forwarded them to each school.

The county office staff see the nature of questions asked and interviews as one means of communicating county office expectations to the schools. Over time, the PIR has served as a source of information for the revision of the Comprehensive Plan for Special Education and for the identification of inservice training needs.

Thus, the PIR provides a means for information exchange, a tool for needs assessment and a means for reporting the status and quality of programs. County office staff members report that the format may undergo major changes as the issues of concern change with time.

Planning of Individual School Programs

A broad range of perspectives was represented in the planning of a Hopkins, Minnesota, program to curb the dropout and absence rate of mildly and moderately handicapped secondary school youth.

Identification of the need for this program occurred at the secondary school where the program was implemented. Major administrative changes are unnecessary for this strategy. However, an additional organizational structure was created within the school. The goals and operation of this strategy were introduced at school, district, community, and state levels simultaneously.

Those involved in the planning process for this program were administrative personnel, instructional personnel, state education office personnel, community agency representatives, parents, and students. Those groups were involved in planning, writing, collecting data, and assisting in formulating the program.

The actual planning process has been documented by the LEA staff following a general systems approach to problem solving, planning, and funding. Of importance is the role which students and community representatives played in conceptualizing and planning this strategy. Participating in the planning were students who had dropped out of school or had been provided guidance services for emotional, behavioral, and learning difficulties. Community representatives included in the planning were two police liaison officers and the president of the local Association for Children with Learning Disabilities. In the last stages of planning, input was solicited from members of the school board, PTA, YMCA, Jewish Family and Children's Service, Mental Health Center, nonpublic education institutions, and the local family and child health service center.

Essentially the planning committee's task was one of program development. This effort led to the writing of a successful funding proposal. Once implementation of the project began, the committee ceased to function as a separate body. Several of the individual participants in the planning process assumed responsibilities on the project staff.

The length of time used in formal planning for this strategy was approximately three months; however, it was estimated that total planning time was six months from the initial identification of need. The overseer, a secondary counselor who later became the program director, was given compensatory leave for the time spent in planning.

The program that resulted emphasized educational and counseling intervention directed at students, parents, and teachers. Parents and teachers were included in response to the underlying assumption that change in student behavior depends not only on change in the student's environment, but also in response to the level and quality of support which they receive from parents, teachers, and peers. In addition to benefiting from the development of a needed program, the district benefited from having a well-informed cadre of professionals who could apply their newfound knowledge to this program and to broader educational programs for all students. This is a fine example of experimental learning which can have individual benefits as well.

Summary: Planning

Two elements necessary for effective and efficient planning have been discussed here: a range of knowledgeable key personnel and time. The strategies presented in this section have addressed these elements, exemplifying the proposition that proper incentives for participation, enough time for information gathering and reporting, and a structured planning process maximize the amount of information obtained and facilitate effective planning.

ACQUIRING AND ALLOCATING RESOURCES

Resources are generally measured in terms of manpower, money, materials, equipment, and facilities. They represent the direct costs of operating programs. Even though education for handicapped students has been receiving a larger share of federal dollars, the constraints faced by local education agencies still make it difficult to provide all services in various settings to meet handicapped students' needs. Some of these constraints arise from specific state appropriations legislation while others result from conflicts between federal requirements and local procedures. The following strategies describe methods that have been used by local education agencies to provide more flexibility in allocating funds.

IEP Contingency Fund

Rather than requesting a specified number of service providers for the following year, special education administrators in New Braunfels, Texas, have found it more cost effective to request a sum of money which can be allocated for staff as needs unfold.

The idea of an IEP Contingency Fund was a new, more flexible concept of funding for anticipated services. The Budget Committee approved such a fund, but allocated much less than had previously been allotted for special service providers.

A planning committee consisting of the director of special education, the assistant superintendent of elementary education, the assistant superintendent of secondary education and the deputy superintendent was formed to develop the finer aspects of the contingency fund plan. Issues such as the appropriate budget line for this item and guidelines for application and approval of funds were discussed. This work was performed over a two-week period during the summer.

A permanent committee comprised of the director of special education, assistant supervisor of elementary education and assistant supervisor of secondary education was then formed to insure that the following process was used. *Requests for additional staff are submitted for review.* Any teacher may submit a request as long as it is documented by a student's IEP. Program coordinators occasionally submit requests jointly with teachers, although principals rarely submit requests.

There are several intermediate steps before an application reaches the committee. A group meeting of all parties affected by the need is held. They prioritize needs in relation to existing programs. If at all possible, an attempt is made to meet the need within the system. For example, staff could be re-allocated. If it is not possible to meet the need, then the need is documented and a written request is submitted to the committee for review.

The committee meets four times a year to review requests. It has its own set of standards for the review of requests, including consideration of the number of students in the existing program, the amount of service that will be supplied to students, and the relation of the request to mainstreaming goals. A request for additional services is not likely to be refused.

However, committee members reported that if a request is refused, the person submitting the request can appeal in person. A letter stating the reason for refusal always accompanies denial of a request. If a request is granted, the deputy superintendent signs the request.

Perhaps the most difficult step is finding people to fill new positions. Many people are unwilling to work without a contract and there is not a surplus of qualified service providers in this area. Sometimes, much of the year will pass before staff can be found. Another problem is that all positions terminate at the end of the year due to funding patterns. If the service needs to be continued, a new request must be submitted at the beginning of the year.

This process was explained to principals individually and through a newsletter. However, they reported being unaware of the appeals procedure. Lack of direct communication with the committee was the principals' greatest criticism of this strategy.

Advantages of this strategy are that the process requires the district to prioritize services offered to students. It is also cost efficient: many needs are met by better use of existing staff. Because of this, the contingency fund is rarely used.

State Reimbursement Option

Often, states that reimburse local districts according to personnel units do so either on a straight sum or percentage basis. Most states using the percentage formula also include a maximum ceiling for each position. As staff seniority and salaries increase, the ceiling often results in some districts receiving less than the authorized percentage.

Existing legislation in Minnesota provides flexible funding for vocational education for handicapped students. Administrators may choose to charge personnel costs for vocational education to either vocational or special education if the instructors are certified in both areas. Since vocational and special education are funded under different formulas, this option allows program administrators to choose the most beneficial formula. A bill before the legislature has been proposed to make this option available for all special education costs.

The obvious outcome is that the school district would receive the maximum amount. Also, since the amount reimbursed to the local district could be increased if instructors hold dual certification, there is more incentive for instructors to pursue dual certification in vocational and special education.

Comparison of Resource Allocation Strategies

A common purpose of these resource allocation strategies is to allow greater flexibility for changing special education needs. The IEP contingency fund procedures have two advantages: they assure that the need for services cannot be met by reallocation of current staff and they require the district to prioritize its service needs. State funding formula options, in addition to providing flexibility, offer an incentive for teachers to obtain dual certification.

Since more students with a wider range of service needs are entering the education system and greater variety in placement exists, staff needs and other resource needs are apt to shift more rapidly. Flexibility in allocating resources is a major benefit under these conditions.

CONCLUSION

The expansion of the special education domain during the last decade was precipitated by state and federal legislation and has presented a challenge to local education agency administrators concerned with the provision of a free, appropriate education in least restrictive environments to the handicapped students in our nation's schools. Expanding requirements for special education services and resources have demanded new, more effective ways for managing service allocation. Administrators are now challenged not only to administer the LEA programs set in motion to meet the newly defined constituency, but also to offer a finely delineated continuum of service options which may be considered when selecting each student's educational environment(s).

Throughout this chapter, an effort has been made to present administrative and delivery system strategies which facilitate the education of handicapped students in most appropriate environments. These strategies represent local education agencies' responses to the expanded special education domain and to the organizational changes necessitated by state and federal legislation. The exploration of such administrative issues becomes increasingly important as local education agencies develop organizational methods for dealing with increased complexities, new constraints, and innovative alternatives.

Each section of this chapter has addressed different dimensions of the administrator's concerns regarding program implementation and management. The strategies presented in these sections, like all strategies detailed throughout the book, must be viewed as prototypes which may be adapted to fit individual district characteristics and needs. The following discussions address the adaptation of the strategies presented in each section.

Strategies to Streamline the Referral to Placement Process

The first section of this chapter, streamlining the referral to placement process, discussed systematically applied organizational modifications to established classification procedures. Methods for reducing the overload of special education referrals and associated paperwork are presented in the sections on prereferral services and streamlined evaluation/assessment procedures.

Prereferral Services

Prereferral strategies make us more aware of the numerous options which must not be overlooked in planning individualized student programs to maximize the integration of handicapped children with their nonhandicapped peers. This section presented both team approaches to prereferral, which emphasize the coordination of multidisciplinary perspectives, and individual approaches to prereferral, which highlight the ongoing, consultative function of these persons for regular educators.

This section on streamlining the referral to placement process suggests that by redefining and expanding the boundaries of the special education service delivery system to include classroom teachers and other pertinent staff, the local education agencies have not only eased the burden placed on the system by greater numbers of referrals and evaluations, but have also improved the skills of classroom teachers in working with handicapped students. The future of educating handicapped students in most appropriate, least restrictive environments is enhanced by these local education agency endeavors to such a degree that, given time and continued assistance, classroom teachers will be better able to work with handicapped students without fear of failure or frustration.

These strategies also reflect the value of peer consultation processes, which, when properly applied, initiate and strengthen teacher growth. This process not only produces growth in terms of teacher competency, but also reinforces the philosophical tenet that mildly handicapped students should be educated, whenever possible, in regular education settings.

All of the strategies to streamline the referral to placement process are adaptable to a variety of LEA-SEA organizational arrangements. The generic teacher is the most widely applicable strategy of this type since it is adaptable across all types of administrative structure. It does, however, require personnel to be specially trained for the role. All of the strategies in this category could be easily used in urban or small areas; the learning team model could also be easily used where school buildings are widely dispersed. All streamlining models except the building screening committee could be implemented in LEAs experiencing a space shortage.

Strategies in this category require coordination both within buildings and within classrooms. Only two strategies, the generic teacher and the child study teams, also require coordination at the district level. The most costly of the three procedures to institute is the generic teacher; these costs reflect the addition of salaries and fringe benefits to the budget. The four teaming strategies may be quickly implemented while the generic teacher strategy requires time for defining the role, recruiting qualified personnel, and preparing current district staff for implementation of the new role.

Overall, while the use of various combinations of teams offers diversity in personnel usage and quick start-up time, the generic teacher model could actually be implemented successfully under the most challenging circumstances. However, this latter strategy is expensive, time-consuming, and requires specifically trained personnel, while team approaches generally use personnel currently employed within the district.

Strategies to Streamline Assessment/Evaluation Procedures

The second part of this section presented strategies to assist in streamlining evaluation and assessment procedures. These strategies emphasized both team and individual approaches with decentralization of responsibilities for persons involved in assessment roles. Each of these strategies was unique; each offered differing benefits. Appraisal teams provided teachers with detailed educational plans; diagnostic teams offered student counseling services. The evaluation team chairperson, as an administrator, monitored and coordinated the evaluation to placement process. The purpose of these strategies was similar, however, in that all were designed to expedite the formal evaluation and assessment process.

Each of the strategies discussed in this section may be easily used within a variety of administrative structures and in urban or small LEAs. However, the diagnostic team strategy would be difficult to use in districts that have a shortage of space, since it requires rooms within schools where assessment personnel may work.

Although these strategies are suitable for use within many districts, they have different requirements for implementation. The appraisal team requires district-wide coordination; the evaluation team chairperson needs coordination of activities within a school building; and the diagnostic team requires both district-level and classroom-level coordination in order to assure appropriate service delivery. All three strategies require some change in personnel. New personnel are needed for the appraisal team while the other two strategies may be successfully implemented by reassigning or transferring presently employed personnel. Both the evaluation team chairperson and the diagnostic team need ongoing support and staff development; the appraisal team concept may be adapted with little staff development. The implementation of all strategies to streamline assessment procedures requires substantial funds, primarily for salaries. The least expensive of these is the evaluation team chairperson. Planning and implementing each of these strategies is a lengthy process.

In selecting a strategy from this category, the administrator must carefully consider the purpose for using a team or person. The appraisal team uses new personnel to perform innovative functions. The diagnostic team offers a classroom-level model with reassigned district personnel. The use of an evaluation team chairperson to centralize the assessment procedure provides clear coordination of each student's comprehensive assessment. Thus, each model presents a different profile which should be compared to the LEA's characteristics to determine its applicability.

Strategies to Manage an Increased Workload

The second section of the chapter dealt with managing an increased workload. These strategies are of two types. An increased administrative workload may be managed through the implementation of strategies to improve time utilization. This may be accomplished by conducting time management studies and providing workshops on efficient time usage. An increased workload may be dealt with by using computers to process the enormous amounts of data which administrators are required to have at their immediate disposal.

Strategies to Improve Time Utilization

Some of the difficulties brought about by increased administrative workloads can be ameliorated by more efficient use of time. However, better use of time often presents a problem for all school personnel. In this section, three ways to improve personnel time usage were discussed. Two of these strategies outlined workshops which were presented to improve time management while one explored a study to document actual time spent in activities by teachers.

Among the three strategies noted in this section, only the time utilization survey could be easily implemented across all administrative structures. Building space was not a consideration in selecting these strategies since most school districts have large rooms available to conduct these training activities.

While the administrators' workshop requires coordination only at the district level and the teachers' workshop requires it only at the building level, implementation of the time utilization study requires coordination at both of these levels. The study also requires new personnel. Staff development and support are required at the consultation level to maintain skills learned in the two workshops and intensive, long-term staff development is required to train data collectors for the time utilization study. The study requires substantial funds for a short period of time, the workshop for teachers requires minimal funds, and the administrators' workshop requires no new funding. Of the three, only the study requires a lengthy implementation period.

Overall, then, it seems that these strategies are closely linked and designed to meet the needs of two groups. The time utilization study was conducted to obtain information on teachers' uses of time in one LEA; that process provided the basis for the workshop on effective time usage. While the study was relatively expensive and time-consuming as well as requiring a great deal of intradistrict coordination, it provided a practical, logical, and relevant means to encourage change. Plans based on the study were drawn to assist the teachers from whom data had been collected. Contrastingly, the administrators' workshop was built on general principles of time management for these personnel.

Strategies to Use Computers

Since the timely snythesis and retrieval of information form the basis for program planning and resource allocation, strategies directed toward managing data were presented in the third part of this section. First, strategies for using existing computer systems to maintain data on handicapped students were presented. Second, a process of contracting for special education information was detailed. The first option may be exercised when an LEA possesses the capital and qualified personnel needed to develop, maintain, and update an in-house computer system. In contrast, the second option, that of contracting, may be successfully used by districts whose own computers are currently filled or whose information needs are less than those required to justify the cost of implementing an entire information management system in one district. Shared computer costs among several districts is a variation of this option.

While many local education agencies presently use computer facilities to collate, categorize, and analyze information, the potential of computer assisted information management has not yet been reached. In the future, advancing technologies and greater awareness of computer capabilities should result in better use of available software packages.

All computer strategies described within this chapter may be easily implemented regardless of the administrative structure of the LEA. While Contra Costa's system required many highly trained personnel, Arlington's MIS could be implemented with a shortage of district personnel since theirs was a contracted service. The Dallas system could be used under either condition; however, it, too, would seem most appropriate if trained personnel were readily available.

The system used in Dallas requires only within-district coordination while the Arlington system also requires community coordination and the Contra Costa MIS also calls for within-building coordination. Since Arlington contracted for computer services, no change in the roles of district staff was needed; both of the other systems needed new personnel with data management skills. Arlington's system required no staff development, Dallas' required ongoing consultation, and Contra Costa's required long-term staff development to instruct teachers on how to use the system. The implementation of all three information management systems required substantial funds. The contractual services used by Arlington allow for quick strategy implementation, while a district implementing an MIS on its own may anticipate a lengthy planning and implementation period.

Overall, the MIS strategies address different needs. Arlington needed a system to supplement their existing capabilities. Therefore, the quickest solution was provided through the use of a contractual arrangement. The Dallas system provided a centrally located and staffed research department which provided information and conducted studies on request. The Contra Costa system represented the most comprehensive system in that teachers and principals were taught to use the MIS and encouraged to add or access data from their building-based terminals. These characteristics and the focus of each system should be important concerns to LEAs seeking to implement management information systems.

Planning Strategies

In the third section of the chapter, models for program planning were presented. These strategies embody the philosophy that two elements are essential in planning processes. The first of these is well-trained personnel who represent a variety of perspectives. The second essential planning element is time to analyze, define, and outline each task to be initiated in achieving desired educational goals. The strategies represent several models for accomplishing district goals while assuring personnel the time needed to synthesize their ideas throughout the planning process.

These planning strategies successfully demonstrated that there are methods through which administrators may expand the decision-making body to include key personnel and to provide the time needed for comprehensive planning. Sound planning strategies attempt to address a wide variety of needs, opinions, and demands in order to allocate resources in a manner which ensures program success. Successful planning strategies, such as those discussed within this chapter, may be characterized by their high degree of participant commitment and follow-through.

The program implementation review, school subcommittees, individual program planning, and planning survey could be easily implemented under most administrative structures, while participatory planning could be most easily used where administrative links were direct and where regular and special education services were coordinated. Participatory planning and school subcommittees could be used in LEAs experiencing a personnel shortage, since planning team members are currently involved in district activities. This was also true of the program planning strategy where school personnel and community members were involved.

The participatory planning strategy would be easily implemented in small districts or geographically separated areas, since the administrator who works with planning personnel may need to travel among sites to conduct planning sessions. No special space requirements are called for with the planning strategies except for room for the participatory planning sessions to be held.

While none of these strategies needs within-classroom coordination, both subcommittees and the planning survey require community, district, and building coordination. Participatory and systems planning require only community and district coordination, while the program implementation review needs within-district and building coordination. All strategies except the program planning may be implemented with no change in the job responsibilities of present district employees; the subcommittee and program planning strategies require ongoing consultation. Since participatory planning involves a college course, substantial funding may be needed to implement the strategy. The program implementation review and program planning may be implemented with minimal funds, while neither of the remaining two planning strategies requires funds for implementation. Since planning procedures usually require a lengthy start-up period, it is not surprising to note that four of the five strategies fit this pattern and that only the participatory planning strategy may be quickly implemented.

Strategies to Acquire and Allocate Resources

The final sections of this chapter dealt with the acquisition and allocation of resources, presenting two ways of distributing resources on the basis of student needs. The section would perhaps be more enlightening and useful to most local education agencies if it offered some panacea to the financial burdens on the special education delivery system. However, school administrators are currently regulated through federal and state legislation to provide services to handicapped students either within the local district or through supplemental services provided by cooperative agreement with other community agencies. It is hoped, however, that the strategies within this chapter will offer incentives for all local education agencies that are faced with similar constraints and contingencies. The remaining chapters of this book contain strategies that are also related to efficient allocation of resources.

Strategies to acquire and allocate resources which are presented in this chapter are designed to ensure appropriate services to handicapped students through the use of alternate personnel funding patterns. The IEP contingency fund may be used in districts which are characterized by direct, uncomplicated administrative structures. The state reimbursement option is useful where the administrative arrangement between the SEA and LEA is direct enough to allow for a clear-cut delineation of criteria to be used in funding dually certified personnel. It is also useful where there is an abundance of trained personnel and in small or urban areas.

While the IEP contingency fund requires coordination within the district, building, and classroom, the state reimbursement option requires coordination only with the SEA. The IEP fund requires the recruitment of new, skilled personnel while the state option requires no change in the current functions of school personnel. The IEP fund requires a minimal level of funding and lengthy implementation while the state option requires no LEA funds and may be quickly employed.

Concluding Comments

Spurred by the impetus of recent state and federal legislation, the expansion of the special education domain has resulted in an increasingly diverse provision of services to a broadened client base. Both regular and special educators are now working together in a coordinated fashion to assure that each student receives a free, appropriate public education in the least restrictive environment. Educators are experiencing success in their efforts to provide timely, relevant services for handicapped students. However, the growing complexity in providing appropriate service is manifested in needs to streamline the referral to placement process, to manage an increased workload, to engage in productive planning, and to acquire needed resources. These tasks demand strategies designed to facilitate the development of practical administrative and delivery systems. The strategies in this chapter represent attempts to address these needs.

Administrative systems are designed to organize the tasks of LEA leaders into manageable components. Their usefulness depends on the degree to which they assist school administrators in balancing the many competing subsystems within an individual LEA. Their responsiveness may be gauged in terms of their flexibility in allowing administrators to monitor and update existing procedures while implementing additional strategies to address newly identified needs.

Delivery systems are organized to provide a cohesive framework within which services provided to handicapped students may be ordered. These systems are designed to assure the delivery of effective, efficient, individually determined instructional and supportive services to all handicapped students. Better planned and more diverse forms of service are being provided increasingly by teams of special and regular educators working in tandem. The merger of regular and special education service delivery systems is now being encouraged through the expansion of the special education domain.

As administrative and delivery systems originally designed for special education become more widely used within the total education system, it seems that the fine demarcation which has traditionally been drawn between these two domains may vanish. Even now, most service delivery systems include the regular education classroom as a special education placement option; indeed, by law, it is the least restrictive environment for many handicapped students currently served in our nation's schools. Strategies presented in this chapter suggest that administrative and delivery systems may form the logical basis for instituting change to support the merger of these two domains so that, through administrators' efforts, a free, appropriate public education may be provided to all students.

REFERENCE

Chalfant, J. C., Pysh, M. V., & Moultrie, R. Teacher assistance teams: A model for within building problem solving. *Learning Disabilities Quarterly*, 1979, *2*, 85, 96.

2

Community Involvement

GEORGE W. SHELLEM

School administrators have responded to the mandate for the delivery of appropriate educational services to handicapped students in the least restrictive environment through a variety of creative and effective strategies. Often administrators have been required to expand the number, characteristics, or intensity of existing programs. While the logistics of such changes fall under the purview of administrative and delivery systems, supplemental resources may be needed to accomplish the required changes. This chapter deals with one resource which often goes untapped: the community.

Historically, local education agencies have been asked to assume a major financial responsibility for establishing and maintaining instructional programs. Monies and other resources needed to support programming efforts most often came from local revenues. However, the expanding scope of present-day programming efforts requires school administrators to seek additional means to support new programs. One of these means is through the coordinated use of community resources and the increased use of community members as partners in the educational process.

Administrators have reconsidered a variety of resources which are available for these purposes. Resources necessary to support program development and expansion have been made available through several sources. Among these are: (a) the allocation of additional monies for special education, (b) a more effective utilization of existing internal resources, and (c) the utilization of external community resources.

This chapter explores the uses of external resources to meet the educational needs of mildly handicapped children in the least restrictive environment, for example, to increase the number of program service options, the quality of service, and the feasibility of less restrictive placements. After a brief discussion of the rationale and critical considerations for using external resources, an organizational scheme is presented to define and describe various types of strategies for using those resources. Then, a description of actual implemented strategies illustrates their effective use. The chapter closes with a summary of other potential uses of interagency agreements and strategies for involving the community in the educational process.

THE NEED FOR SUPPLEMENTAL RESOURCES

The need for additional resources for the wider array of programs and services called for by Public Law 94-142 and Section 504 of the Rehabilitation Act of 1973 has encouraged local educational agencies to design strategies which utilize previously untapped community resources, including those available through other public or private organizations and agencies. One example of increased pressure to use external resources is the recent ruling by the court in *Armstrong v. Kline* (476 F. Supp. 583 [E.D. Pa 1979]) which established that inflexible standards in state department of education regulations violate the provisions of Public Law 94-142 and Section 504 of the Rehabilitation Act of 1973. The court, in overturning inflexible regulations which limit programming without consideration of unique needs, has provided administrators with a huge task. For example, the 180-day school year is often in conflict with the educational needs of certain severely handicapped children who regress considerably during the summer months. For the schools to respond to this ruling by utilizing only internal resources would severely cut into their financial base and could result in limiting regular school year programs. Strategies to provide additional schooling without adversely affecting regular programs have been developed with assistance, cooperation, and support from external sources.

Although the direct responsibility for implementing the federal mandate falls on only one of society's institutions—the schools—the law is actually a mandate for all of society. The schools lack the financial base to completely implement the law; however, they bear the obligation to do so. Special education is costly, especially when supportive and related services are required in addition to the special education program. Because of the range and variety of services needed and because only small numbers of students may require these services, it is often not economical for the school system to act autonomously in providing them. Whereas the cost of hiring a full time psychologist to work with the school system may be economically unwarranted, the use of existing community mental health agencies as the provider of services is not. Thus, sole use of internal funding to support educational services for the handicapped is not a feasible solution—it is accompanied by the risk of inappropriate, fragmented services, and an unfulfilled goal of educational equality.

The complexity of the problem is further increased by the least restrictive environment provision of the mandate. Local school administrators are required to provide appropriate educational services which meet the unique needs of the individual child in an educational setting that promotes interaction with nonhandicapped children to the maximum extent appropriate and, when possible, to educate the handicapped child in the school nearest his or her home. Saving dollars by grouping handicapped children categorically in segregated facilities (regardless of individual learning styles) is no longer an acceptable option, since the least restrictive environment provision calls for a continuum of placement options for handicapped children.

A CATEGORIZATION OF SUPPLEMENTAL RESOURCES

There are a number of ways one can categorize the problems associated with the provision of a free, appropriate public education in the least restrictive environment; strategies to address these problems may also be categorized in a variety of ways. Prior to delineation of the categories used in this chapter, however, we will operationally define certain terms. The basic approach of the chapter is taken from organizational theory: education is seen as an open system that interacts with its environment.

The local education agency is considered a complete entity in and of itself, with permeable boundaries separating the agency and its environment. Any resource that is outside of LEA parameters is defined as an external resource; this includes other educational agencies and institutions which are not inherently linked to the LEA. Resources can be made available from a variety of external sources, including other public agencies, private individuals, and foundations.

Within this chapter, distinctions between internal and external funding sources are based on the active efforts required of a school district to obtain funds. For example, state funding guaranteed under basic foundation support or equalization formulas is considered an internal resource because it is an accepted and integral part of the financial base of education. However, other state resources that are not guaranteed and are allocated on the basis of need are considered external resources. Incentive grants and the participation of a state department specialist in an inservice effort are examples of external state resources. These are limited resources that are allocated on the basis of an identified need and are obtained through the active efforts of the school district working independently of other school districts. The school district is motivated by concerns for its own organizational stability, and is not working as a coordinated component of the total state-wide educational system.

The use of external resources is based on a larger planning or resource base in order to gain economy of scale. Services for low incidence handicapped populations are not cost effective unless a minimum base can be provided. By entering into cooperative arrangements with other school districts, the appropriate services can be provided at more reasonable costs. The purpose of these arrangements is not to maximize the available resources, but rather to minimize the costs associated with providing the service. Often the initial or base costs of certain programs are constant, regardless of the number of students. Under Public Law 94-142, the "State educational agency is responsible for insuring that each educational program for handicapped children administered within the state, including each program administered by any other public agency: (i) is under the general supervision of the persons responsible for educational programs for handicapped children in the State educational agency, and (ii) meets the education standards of the State educational agency (including the requirements of this part)" (34 CFR §300a.600).

Under Section 504, the primary recipient carries the responsibility to provide a free, appropriate public education to handicapped individuals. Although they must bear the responsibility for meeting these mandates, school districts can cooperate to provide the necessary services. Such cooperation can lower per pupil costs and better distribute associated fixed costs.

Often the logical delivery system is through other agencies or organizations in the community. In such cases, the school's internal resources can go directly to the service provider or can be used in combination with community resources.

Throughout this chapter, a distinction is made between the use of community resources and interagency agreements or cooperation. The term community resources refers to fiscal, material, and human resources that exist within the local environment that surrounds the school system. A community resource could be adaptive park equipment purchased by the town but available for use by the school, community volunteers used as aides or program assistants, or private or public speech and hearing clinics used for evaluation and assessment. The key differentiation between the use of community resources and interagency cooperation is the formality of the arrangements. Although the community resource may be made available by sharing the materials or personnel of two agencies, a document delineating the terms of the agreement and conditions is not developed. Interagency cooperation, on the other hand, implies a formal agreement specifying the services to be provided by each party and binds the parties contractually.

Interagency agreements result in part from the accountability that each unit has to its customers and constituents for appropriate use of allocated resources. Since services or resources are diverted from direct application to the agency's legislated or commonly recognized clientele, a means of accounting for resources and the benefits derived from their use is essential. Often, instead of one agency's resources being used by another, a working relationship between two agencies to more effectively serve common clientele is developed. Another variation is a relationship that allows one agency to provide resources directly but also allows the use of facilities, personnel, or the delivery system of a second agency.

Interagency cooperation includes administrative agreements which allocate resources to programs serving a new clientele group, provide a streamlined service delivery system, combine resources to maximize service delivery, or clarify the agency/client relationship to reduce duplication of services. Although there may be some exchange of funds, there is no direct purchase of services. Such arrangements are contractual and represent a third major type of strategy available for obtaining needed services. A school that contracts for a service is purchasing that service as it would any other resource that is not internally available. Although schools depend heavily on contracts for material and equipment acquisition, schools have not readily used this strategy as a means for acquiring human services (except in the areas of medical services and major equipment repair). Most often this strategy is used when the service is of short duration or directed to a small population or when the services are required intermittently or sporadically. Since most school administrators are already familiar with the implications and advantages of contractual arrangements, only selected strategies of this type are presented in the chapter. These strategies represent nontraditional approaches to service delivery through contractual arrangements.

This chapter is organized according to these three types of community resources, which form a continuum from informal to formal. One pole of the continuum is community resources that require informal commitment. The formal end of the continuum is represented by contractual arrangements which legally bind both parties to the terms contained in the agreement. Between the two poles, somewhat closer to the formal one, are interagency agreements.

Although this continuum is based on the formality of the agreements, other characteristics of the agreements generally vary in accordance with the degree of formality. These include the amount of time necessary to establish the relationship, amount of time required for planning, extent of commitment required by parties to the agreement, duration of services, and the flexibility or latitude that exists in the agreement. Administrators searching for long term solutions to significant problems may be more comfortable with formal arrangements, since stability is assured.

The strategies presented reflect approaches to solving problems generated by schools' attempts to serve mildly handicapped children in the least restrictive environment; in addition, some strategies emphasize the development of community support. The strategies will be discussed under three specific headings: community resources, interagency agreements, and contractual arrangements.

As was indicated earlier, the purpose of this handbook is not to provide detailed instructions on the use of strategies, but rather to provide examples of strategies in these categories which focus on a variety of problems. It is hoped that the chapter can be a means for enhancing a creative problem solving approach characterized by openness to variety of alternatives which include the use of resources available from both internal and external sources.

UTILIZATION OF COMMUNITY RESOURCES

In recent years, the concept of community education has gained increased support among educators and community leaders. They feel that the schools belong to the community and that valuable resources and facilities are not fully utilized when school buildings sit locked and vacant from 3:30 p.m. until 8:30 a.m. Likewise, the inability of school personnel to utilize other private and public resources may result in inadequate service delivery or needless duplication of resources, materials, and/or equipment. This section of the chapter focuses on strategies that maximize use of existing community resources.

Strategies in this group are simple arrangements. Many were developed by individuals and require no formal agreements or delineation of terms. Some strategies were developed by educational systems seeking additional resources; others resulted from attempts by the community at large to meet social or recreational needs through cooperation with educational programs. All, however, require clear definition of the desired objective by all parties and a mutual examination of available resources that may be brought to bear on that objective. Since the aim of these strategies is to maximize the use of existing resources and to broaden the participation of the community in the lives of handicapped children, the interaction that occurs between handicapped and nonhandicapped persons often results in unforeseen benefits.

In this section, six strategies are discussed. The first three describe ways in which community resources can be used to provide services directly to the students. The remaining three exemplify use of individuals from the community to assist in program planning and to perform such administrative tasks as needs identification and program evaluation.

Community Recreational Resources

The recreational and leisure time needs of handicapped children cannot be adequately met by a program limited to school hours. Communities throughout the country have, in recent years, expanded opportunities for nonhandicapped children to engage in recreational, social, and leisure time activities through programs sponsored and funded by tax dollars. In these programs, participation of handicapped children must be fostered and revisions in format, style, or material may be required in order to enable handicapped children to participate fully in the experience.

One community that has developed such a program is the town of Arlington, Massachusetts. The program provides a wide range of educational, recreational, and social activities to handicapped citizens of all ages, preschool through adult. The auxiliary aids, support, and personnel necessary to ensure optimal involvement in and benefit from the experience are provided through the mutual efforts of the school and community. At first, handicapped children are involved in specially developed and segregated programs. As they gain experience, they are better able to participate in integrated activities, since they have acquired prerequisite skills. The program uses existing facilities of both the town parks and recreation department and the school system. Cooperating school officials transport the children on city buses to the sites of after school activities. Transportation for citizens with ambulatory aids is available through the recreation department's Handi-Dart, a specially equipped van. Recreational facilities and playground equipment are routinely shared by the schools and the town.

In addition, special education teachers assist staff of a community summer camp by providing inservice training, materials, and informal input. Efforts are under way to expand this cooperation and to provide summer camp staff with behaviorally stated objectives derived from actual IEPs. This sharing of information and materials allows for program consistency and the special services which greatly facilitate the continued and uninterrupted growth of the child.

In summary, the recreation department's philosophy of viewing the leisure time needs of handicapped citizens as being essentially no different from the needs of other community members has resulted in a variety of innovative ways for increasing the accessibility of recreational activities. An important point that must be stressed is that the Arlington Special Needs Recreational Program provides a flexible balance of integrated and segregated programming. Separate programming is important, especially for adolescents and older handicapped citizens who did not have the opportunity to participate in many of these activities when they were younger. But once they acquire rudimentary skills and self-confidence, they can then participate in regular recreational programs. Other means of integrating handicapped and nonhandicapped citizens arise when the Special Needs Program sponsors special events which are open to the entire community. Such "reverse mainstreaming" activities are beneficial as a means of educating the community to the needs and capabilities of their handicapped neighbors.

A first step in implementing such a program is to involve a number of key individuals from the school, community, and parent or consumer groups. Efforts should build on recreational and arts and crafts activities already existing in the schools. Initial efforts might prove easier to implement if the focus is on large scale projects, such as a summer camp, or a number of special events, such as Special Olympics, or day trips.

The Arlington program had its roots in a summer camp that was established for mentally retarded children. It was a definable population that had obvious needs and provided clear parameters within which a summer camp program could be developed. The success of the program led members of the special education department, parents, and others to expand the program to include after-school activities during the school year. Projects that are definable and have clear start and end points help to focus the energy of the community. Once the commitment of the community has been received through a number of successful projects like these, it is much easier to extend support to activities that are less clearly defined, because the programs have gained credibility.

The Arlington Special Needs Recreation Program is funded entirely by the town of Arlington, as part of its overall recreation and parks budget. The town receives a 50% reimbursement from the state for the special needs program. The town has hired a full time recreational therapist to design, develop, and manage the Special Needs Program. Since its inception, the position of recreation therapist has been funded through CETA monies; however, it could also be funded as a regular town position. The program also makes extensive use of volunteers, such as the Arlington Youth Leaders (AYL), an organization jointly sponsored by the Arlington Recreation Department and the local Association for Retarded Citizens.

Since the Arlington school system had already purchased adapted physical education and playground equipment for its own programs, the recreation department has saved the expense of purchasing it. The recreation therapist maintains close liaison with the Arlington Special Education Director in order to minimize duplication as much as possible.

Overall, this program exemplifies a strategy that satisfies the needs of two service providers and the consumer group. Through a comprehensive and well organized after-school, weekend, and summer recreation program, handicapped children are exposed to many learning experiences which will facilitate their in-school learning. As handicapped individuals develop new and expanded skills, their self-images and self-concepts improve. Similarly, the community gains from this cooperative approach since the essential components to a successful program are available through the school system. Adaptive equipment, recreational facilities, and skilled personnel are available to the community. Handicapped children are provided experiences which assist them in becoming part of the community and in sharing experiences which build community spirit. The community, as a whole, gains citizens who are able to participate in community activities and share their wealth of knowledge and experience.

Mental Health Consultation

Mental health professionals who work through the schools are confronted by several constraints which restrict their ability to respond fully to the needs of a child. First, their case loads do not foster extensive as well as intensive interaction with the child and family. Second, because much of what is "acted out" in school has its beginnings in out-of-school relationships, the school mental health professional is often asked to go far beyond professional obligations in order to understand the "whole child." Mental health professionals in the community often have contact with the same children seen by school mental health professionals. By sharing responsibilities and coordinating therapeutic efforts, school and mental health professionals can more effectively meet the children's needs.

The Arlington, Massachusetts, Youth Consultation Center (AYCC) entered into a cooperative relationship with the school system, and the relationship improved both the quality and extent of services available to students requiring assistance. AYCC staff are assigned to the schools' learning teams (described in Chapter 1) which review referrals and evaluations for special education services. AYCC staff contribute valuable evaluation and assessment information regarding out-of-school behavior, problems, or interventions. In addition, the perspective of a nonschool mental health professional is available.

If the AYCC has already worked with the youth or his or her parents, the information obtained can be made part of the evaluation reports, saving the school both time and effort. When services are recommended, the presence of an AYCC staff member allows referrals to incorporate understanding of the roles, responsibilities and resources of school and community agencies. AYCC also receives direct referrals from the school for counseling, thus protecting school counseling personnel from impossible case loads.

The cooperation between school and AYCC enables the school to make referrals for students or their parents which are much more flexible, individualized and appropriate than would be possible if only the resources of the school were available. Counseling can be made available to parents at times convenient to them. Students also can attend counseling either during school hours or after school, depending on their own specific needs and schedules.

Thus, AYCC representation on the learning team provides consistent and comprehensive counseling and mental health services to Arlington youth, ensures that a broad perspective is available during the evaluation process, facilitates the development of a more complete view of the child, and reduces miscommunication and duplication of services.

The implementation of this strategy does not require elaborate planning, extensive resource investment, or additional equipment or facilities. What it requires is recognition by professionals of the inherent limitations of existing fragmented service delivery systems and the advantages to be gained from cooperative teamwork. The strategy requires an inherent trust and understanding of the roles and responsibilities of other professionals and the importance of working with the "whole child."

The center is mandated to serve Arlington teenagers and their parents without charge and is funded completely by town funds. The staff of about 25 includes several interns from area universities and colleges. Learning team meetings, which are scheduled on a weekly basis, require approximately one to two hours. In addition, the time of AYCC staff members may be required in school referral, evaluation, and assessment.

To cite personnel or time as costs of this strategy is somewhat misleading, since both staff and time are committed to serving the needs of the child. Actually, resources are saved by both the school district and the community health agency by the increased coordination of services and the reduction of duplication.

It must be emphasized that this is not a contractual arrangement. This strategy emanated from informal contacts and shared concern for increased effectiveness of service delivery by the two separate agencies. It represents the pooled talents and resources of two agencies that have overlapping responsibilities and common interests in the child.

The inclusion of AYCC staff on learning teams has been a successful strategy that has resulted in benefits that exceeded even the original intent. Overall, because of the interaction and communication among service providers, resources are utilized much more effectively. The profile developed on each student is much broader, since the student's out-of-school life, family, and home conditions are shared with school personnel. The message given to Arlington youth by different service providers is much more consistent, services can be much more comprehensive, and duplication can be avoided. A forum for discussing concerns, problems, and issues has been established and members are willing to listen to others.

Interagency Communication

Most communities have a variety of social service agencies. Because the service needs of handicapped children often involve several agencies, coordination of services can be difficult. Duplication of service, misunderstanding, and territorial feuds can occur.

The Galveston, Texas, Independent School District has made an attempt to improve service delivery to children by increasing communication and cooperation between agencies through a series of meetings called interagency staffings. The biweekly meetings include volunteers representing six social agencies and the school district, who discuss one to three individual cases. A group leader is chosen for each meeting, and it is the leader's responsibility to select cases to be discussed. Other individuals who are involved with the students are often invited to attend and share their information with the group. As the case is discussed, group members describe their agency's role in the case. Thus, agency representatives develop awareness of the roles and responsibilities of the other agencies as well as sharing vital information important in helping the individual client. When duplication is evident, the members can work out a mutually acceptable solution that ensures continued service delivery without wasting resources. In situations where the needs of the student are not being met, a plan for meeting the student's needs is formulated.

No resources other than members' time are necessary for this strategy. In fact, the strategy saves resources and time because resources are used more effectively, people know whom to contact in other agencies, and a sense of trust and cooperation is developed.

As a result of such group meetings, lines of communication have been established between these local service agencies. Previous misunderstandings have been clarified, duplication of services has been avoided, and gaps in service delivery have been closed. As members of the various agencies gain respect and trust for each other, their commitment and support for handicapped children has grown. Members support each other and assist other agencies, making the coordinated delivery of service to children a much easier task.

Citizens As Volunteers

The educational system is a reflection of the community's goals and values. Since the goals of the educational system are developed in conjunction with the community, it is appropriate that the community be involved evaluating the program. By involving a randomly selected group of citizens to examine the areas of curriculum, finance, facilities, and ancillary services, the Columbia-Brazoria, Texas, school system gains valuable information for program decisions.

This involvement of citizens in program evaluation efforts, which occur every five years, enables two important objectives to be met. First, needed information on programs is compiled without making extensive demands on personnel. Second, community members gain a new perspective on the educational program for handicapped students, a perspective developed through direct and personal contact.

The Citizen School Study Team, by investigating the priorities and goals established by the school district, helps to establish a bond between school and community not found in many areas. An atmosphere of trust and openness is projected by the school district. Also, when the study recommendations are used to justify budget requests or to substantiate program success, support has already been established in the community.

The Citizen School Study Team is composed of 72 citizens randomly selected to represent the district's population distribution by geographical area, ethnic/racial composition, economic distribution, sex, age, and length of residence. In addition, community members selected must have an interest in education and youth as well as a willingness to serve as a member of the study team. The district employs evaluation consultants to assist in organizing the committee and to provide technical assistance to the committee during the process. The Board of Education, the consultants, and the Superintendent of Schools clarify the purpose of the study, specific areas to address, the role of the committee and consultants, and all procedures. The committee and the task forces are then responsible for planning the data collection and analysis.

No real procedural or organizational changes are necessary for this strategy to be implemented; all that is required is a commitment from members of the board of education and school administration to an open examination of their program by citizens.

Since community members volunteer their time, the only cost to the school is the salary of the professional consultants and the time to assemble information packages for the citizen evaluation team. The committee is composed of community members, so there is no need to acquaint them with background information which would be needed by other external evaluators.

The use of the Citizen Study Team allows the Columbia-Brazoria Independent School District to compile and analyze an enormous amount of information, and to have the work performed by individuals possessing a variety of perspectives on education. The district receives both a report of the current status of the schools and future program recommendations. It also has provided 72 members of the community an intense and personal view of the school program. The process has developed valuable community support. The understanding and insight gained by these citizens is shared with countless others throughout the community and has firmly anchored the school program in the community.

Parental Involvement in Program and Policy Evaluation

Rather than hiring consultants to perform an evaluation of their programs and policies, the Spring Branch Independent School District in Texas hired a single consultant to train a variety of school personnel and other individuals. The evaluation team was composed of regular educators, counselors, office personnel, and health service personnel representing the school district, and parents of both handicapped and nonhandicapped children. Since these individuals did not possess experience as program evaluators, a consultant experienced in evaluation design was hired to design the evaluation, to provide evaluation forms, and to design and conduct a workshop for members of the evaluation team. Once the evaluation team understood their roles and the process, they spent one full week evaluating each school in the district.

Like the citizen's school study strategy, this one requires openness and willingness to permit persons external to the school to have full access to information regarding the programs. Adequate time is required to prepare persons unsophisticated in formal evaluation methodology and to develop reporting instruments and procedures. It is also important to put together a team of individuals with varied backgrounds and open minds. Members of the team should clearly understand their roles, the evaluation process and the objectives of the evaluation to insure consistency in results. Hiring a consultant to assist the team in its task and to provide training and technical assistance is an important component of the strategy.

As with the citizen school study strategy, resource commitment is minimal, except for the cost of an external consultant and staff members' time away from regularly assigned duties. The evaluation effort was relatively inexpensive, especially when viewed in terms of the information received by the school district.

The use of multidisciplinary team involving professionals and nonprofessionals, regular and special educators, and parents of handicapped children was valuable in two ways. It enabled the school district to gain objective measurements and also conveyed to staff and community that the school district was serious in meeting the needs of its handicapped students, that it was open to criticism, and that it was willing to involve the community in the development of program decisions. Parents obtained an intensive and comprehensive view of the educational program. This sharing of information through participation in the study and the information gained from the team's report facilitated the establishment of community support. This proved beneficial later, when school officials had to justify expenses for necessary facility modification and renovation to more adequately serve its handicapped students.

Community Involvement in Program Planning

Because schools affect their communities, community members may make important contributions to the development of program goals, objectives, and program design. The Lynnfield, Massachusetts, School District found that the input and information made available by community members was useful in the development of program plans. District administrators resolved what appeared to be an internal school problem with information and direction offered by individuals external to the school.

The situation involved the school's suspension policy. This policy's effect on the community was evidenced when Lynnfield police officials noticed a direct relationship between student suspensions and increases in daytime vandalism and illegal entry. In addition, other problems were associated with the suspension policy. Educators were concerned because a disproportionate number of emotionally handicapped students were among those suspended, posing a dilemma for school administrators. To suspend emotionally handicapped students meant interrupting the educational program that had been specifically designed to remediate their emotional problems. On the other hand, allowing them to stay frustrated alienated instructional staff, who felt that they were not receiving administrative support. Since academic problems often accompany disruptive behavior, the automatic failures that are recorded for every day out on suspension can put a student in a position where academic success is not possible. A student in such a position has no incentive to modify her or his behavior on return to school.

Another problem arises around the relationship of the student's handicapping condition (emotional disturbance) and the behavior which led to the suspension. Can a student so handicapped be suspended without review of the situation by the placement team? Is suspension a change in placement? Although school personnel did not like the school suspension policy, they had no alternative solution until the additional support of community members was directed to the problem. The two groups had different reasons for wanting an alternative solution, but they both agreed that suspending students from school was not changing student behavior.

At the initiation of the chief of police, a group of educators and concerned community members met to discuss the problem and to seek a solution. The interaction of these individuals, who possessed such varying perceptions of the situation, enabled the group to seek strategies which accommodated all relevant concerns. As a result of the meeting, recommendations were developed for an alternative to out-of-school suspensions, and school personnel designed an in-school suspension plan.

The strategy is not so much a formal strategy as it is a reaction. In one sense, it is an example of a school responding to externally generated needs by incorporating community members in the planning process. In another sense, it represents utilization of the perceptions and ideas of community members with diverse backgrounds to contribute to the solution of problems encountered by the school. The important idea in this strategy was not the actual solution to the problem, which was to set up an in-school tutoring system for students instead of sending them home, but the school system's willingness to openly discuss the problem with individuals who were external to the immediate school environment.

Educators must make better use of community members as participants in specific, single focused planning activities. Traditional avenues for community involvement, although important, do not always facilitate interactive problem solving relationships. Such efforts to involve community members in similar activities expand the base of support for the educational system within the community.

Summary: Community Resources

The strategies discussed in this section incorporate a wide variety of community elements and focus on a variety of problems, yet they possess certain traits in common. One distinguishing feature is the informality of the cooperation —the strategies resulted from people getting together and discussing mutual needs or problems and deciding to pool their skills, talents and resources. These strategies reflect the permeability of the boundaries that separate educational institutions from their communities. Little actual money was involved in any of the strategies, yet they established lasting bonds and feelings of partnership in addition to addressing the problems they were designed to solve.

These strategies provide a glimpse of the kinds of specific needs which can be met through the use of community resources. They also delineate in more detail and in sharper focus the gains that can be made when individuals cross the boundaries that separate institutions and seek communication and involvement with others.

Involvement of community members goes a long way toward building a base of community support, but it is also necessary to gain support in order to establish or expand existing community involvement. Parents, agencies, and community members are partners in the educational process with potentially important contributions.

Special education, as a subsystem of education, is dependent on the support of the community to ensure that the resources necessary to meet established goals are provided. Resources for education are limited. Therefore, the more widespread and vocal the support, the greater the likelihood for gaining access to needed resources.

As the sphere of influence of special education widens, the previously strong base of support anchored by parents, educators and advocates of the handicapped must concern itself with developing understanding and awareness of the broader community. The goals, aims, and needs of special education must be shared with and understood by this broader community, a community that consists of educators, parents of nonhandicapped children, and other taxpayers who have an increasing interest in the affairs of special education.

If special educators and advocates for handicapped children are to effectively use the resources of the larger community, they must first develop community awareness of the needs and potentials that exist. They must actively cultivate community support. They must explain and defend the more costly resources necessary to meet the unique educational needs of handicapped children. And they must build bridges which will facilitate communication between special education and the community.

A benefit of the strategies discussed in this section is that they help to create awareness, foster understanding, and provide information, exposure, and experience to community members. Other methods for building support through more formal public relations efforts are addressed in the chapter on communication. The next part of this chapter illustrates more formal interagency agreements and their advantages.

INTERAGENCY AGREEMENTS

In order to provide for the unique individual needs of each handicapped child, a variety of program options is necessary. Both the extent and comprehensiveness of special education services have increased as a result of the federal mandate. Often, these cooperative efforts can be handled informally, as was discussed in the previous section, but sometimes the nature of the agencies involved, the extent of the problem, or the need for accountability to constituent groups requires more formal, legally binding arrangements. Private and public agencies are accountable for the manner in which they use the fiscal, material, and human resources allocated to them; they are also accountable for ensuring that their resources are used both effectively and economically.

Although it is the education agency's responsibility to provide a free, appropriate public education to handicapped children, local education agencies are turning increasingly to other public agencies to assist in delivering services to low incidence populations and to populations of severely and profoundly handicapped students. In addition, they are seeking ways to more effectively provide many of the related services which require a level of specialization and expertise that is uneconomical for a single district to provide. And finally, local education agencies are looking to private and public institutions of higher education for more assistance in the provision of in-service education to both regular and special educators.

The strategies presented in this section illustrate formal arrangements between cooperating agencies. However, although the agencies commit themselves to certain conditions or levels of involvement, these arrangements are different from contracts. Contracts imply an outright purchase of services, whereas interagency agreements reflect a pooling of resources or a clarification of overlapping responsibilities in order to reduce duplication or to compensate for gaps in the provision of services.

A variety of problems can become the focus of interagency agreements. The four strategies presented here are meant only as examples and should not be considered a comprehensive array of possible strategies. They offer a diversity intended to stimulate the creative use of interagency agreements to solve problems.

An Interagency Agreement to Meet Related Service Needs

In order to comply with current federal legislation, school districts must provide a comprehensive program designed to meet individual needs. Necessary program components include preschool screening to facilitate early identification, diagnostic/prescriptive services, and skilled personnel who are capable of administering and scoring tests or conducting psychosocial interviews. Other district needs include consultation and direct services to treat medical, emotional, or behavioral problems.

School districts that are small or rural often have difficulties locating personnel with the needed skills. The Columbia-Brazoria School District in Texas entered into a cooperative agreement with a medical school to provide the necessary services to the children in the district. The agreement assured that these services would be provided, and in return, the medical school would acquire a field training site. The focus of the medical school's involvement was to assist teachers in developing their own skills and resources in dealing with physical, emotional, or behavioral problems.

In addition to direct services provided to students and the consultation and training provided to staff, large scale projects were implemented by the medical school. One such project was the yearly Preschool Round-Up, which assisted the school district with its early identification and screening efforts. The medical school staff trained school district personnel and assisted in conducting the Round-Up.

After initial meetings between district administrators and medical school personnel, an agreement stipulating the conditions for both parties was signed. A liaison was identified for each agency. Visits by medical staff members were regularly scheduled. In addition, consultants from the medical school were assigned to each school in order to ensure continuity and consistency as well as to build trust between school district staff and medical school personnel.

Since the medical school's need for field experience sites was met by this arrangement, the strategy enabled the district to provide a comprehensive service delivery system with minimal resources and at a minimal cost because the service providers were also filling their own needs. As a result of this interagency agreement, highly trained medical personnel are available to meet the needs of the school district for comprehensive service delivery. Had the district relied on its own personnel or contracted for the services, the cost to the district would have been much greater and service delivery may have been hampered.

University Assistance in Program Planning

This strategy describes another cooperative arrangement between a university and a school district, but in the Spring Branch Independent School District in Texas, university personnel are employed as direct instructional service providers to learning disabled adolescents.

A conceptual model for a learning disability program was being finalized at a local university at about the same time the school district recognized its need for such a program. The university staff needed a way to test their model, and the school district was searching for a way to establish a good program. After several tentative and informal meetings between the head of the university program and the district's special education director, it was decided that through cooperation both could achieve their goals. Federal funds were required to implement the program.

Much, if not all, of the program design was conceptualized by the university staff. The model involved four components: a high-intensity learning center, a content mastery program, an essential skills program, and a parents' program.

The model was implemented at a junior high school which had previously been effective in implementing change. However, the first year of implementation proved unsuccessful because too heavy a role was played by the university. Teachers at the junior high never really felt that they were part of the program, since students were transported to the university for the high-intensity learning center. Also, communication avenues were not adequately developed. School district staff felt that they had little ownership of the program or input into it.

Several critical changes were made the second year. The program was more closely identified with the school district—all program components were housed entirely in the school district and teachers at the school were brought into program development. During the summer, they developed special materials for the center, such as talking books and outline books. Finally, resource teachers were involved in a week-long training session prior to the beginning of the school year.

As a result of the changes made in the implementation plan, the program had a much more successful second year. The effort took on more of the characteristics of an interagency agreement, since the resources and involvement required of both institutions were better defined. When compared to the first year, the second year seemed almost like a contractual arrangement.

There are problems with interagency agreements between universities and school districts, and this strategy delineated one of those problems. Often, the university does not realistically perceive the needs of the school district. Unless the school district and university personnel work closely together to ensure that school district personnel share in the "ownership" of the project, chances are that the project will not be successful.

Special Education Cooperatives

As more unserved and underserved handicapped children are identified and individually designed programs are developed to meet their needs, school administrators are finding that district boundaries interfere with the economy of scale necessary for effective and efficient delivery of service in the least restrictive environment. More and more districts are forming special education cooperatives to facilitate the delivery of services to handicapped students.

Cooperatives establish larger planning bases which increase the number of students served and size of the area encompassed. They enable the resources of the member school districts to be more economically focused and assure that appropriate programming does not suffer because an unfair financial burden is placed on each single district. Special education cooperatives do, however, compromise the autonomy traditionally enjoyed by school districts. Since different school districts may have different tax rates and may reflect different community values or expectations for education, cooperative arrangements between districts can become complex and legally intricate. The school districts described here were empowered by state legislation to form a cooperative for both vocational education and special education; each district is required to belong to both.

The five member cooperative's governing board is comprised of active board members of the participating school boards. Representatives serve for three-year terms. In addition to the governing board, there is an executive board composed of superintendents of the participating districts and designated administrators, directors, or supervisors of the cooperative.

The executive board meets monthly and acts as the administering board of the cooperative. To facilitate the administration and supervision of cooperative affairs, the governing board has designated an administrative unit. The administrators and directors of the largest participating district serve as the officers of the cooperative's administrative unit. The assignment of dual responsibilities to these individuals has allowed the cooperative to operate without creating a completely new and separate administrative structure. The administrative unit recruits, supervises, and assigns personnel; manages the fiscal affairs of the cooperative; and audits and reports on the cooperative's activities.

Each of the participating districts is billed monthly for its prorated share of the operating costs of the cooperative. The tenth and final billing for the year is in July and adjusts payments to reflect actual program costs. Cooperative costs are divided into two categories: administrative and capital outlay costs, and operating costs. Administrative and capital outlay costs are shared according to the relative populations of the districts, whereas operating costs are shared on a usage basis.

Cooperative planning and program development is the responsibility of the Special Education Director within the general policy parameters and with the approval of the executive and governing boards. Essentially, the Cooperative Special Education Director serves as the Special Education Director for each participating district.

A cooperative arrangement such as this requires the acknowledgement by school board members of the inadequacies and financial burden created by single district programming for low incidence populations. The investment in facilities, equipment and other associated costs can only be optimized if a stable population requiring these services is ensured. Efforts to explain and describe the benefits which counteract the resulting loss of district autonomy will be essential if support from school board members is to be obtained. Formal and legally binding agreements are essential in order to ensure proper use and disposal of property, equipment, and facilities which belong to the cooperative.

Special education cooperatives differ from arrangements in which one district contracts with another for delivery of services to students. Cooperatives are legal entities empowered to enter into agreements. They represent school district efforts to meet mutual needs through the sharing of resources, require a commitment of resources to a long term effort, and provide an appropriately sized planning base to ensure program stability. Cooperatives can meet general special education needs in rural areas where the scattered population makes special education programs difficult, or they can be focused on meeting the needs of specific subpopulations. The distinguishing feature between cooperatives and contracts for services with other districts is the focus on mutual needs. While there are some drawbacks, a well-conceived cooperative can result in more effective and efficient delivery of services.

Summary: Interagency Agreements

The strategies presented in this section exhibited common characteristics which permitted them to be grouped under the heading of interagency agreements. At the same time, the focus of each strategy was unique. Many other examples of interagency agreements exist. It should be noted that this section included only strategies utilized by local education agencies; no attempt to document or classify agreements between state-level institutions was attempted.

Interagency agreements are by nature more complex and difficult than the other strategies previously discussed. Although the formality, complexity and legality which surround them make them initially less desirable, they are necessary for some problems and needs. As agencies increase in size, they depend more on formal agreements to ensure that all parties involved receive appropriate information regarding the task or activity. Also, because of the size of the material and fiscal resources deployed, participating institutions must receive them through more formal agreements.

Federal legislation requires that expanded services be provided to handicapped children and assigns responsibility to state and local education agencies to ensure that these services are delivered in effective and efficient ways. Because of the additional services necessary to achieve this goal, it is essential that duplication between agencies be reduced and that other agencies not leave the entire problem to the SEAs; local agencies must remain active if the needs of children are to be met.

CONTRACTUAL ARRANGEMENTS FOR UTILIZING COMMUNITY RESOURCES

The basic rationale for using available external resources to meet special education needs is to maximize services provided while maintaining or reducing the level of expenditure. Most strategies discussed in this chapter have involved sharing resources, facilities, or personnel in order to meet the needs of one or both agencies. Such arrangements, whether they were informal or formalized legal agreements, had the effect of clarifying existing agency boundaries in order to streamline service delivery, reduce duplication, or fill an existing gap between agencies. But, in addition, cooperation was evident, and the arrangements facilitated more effective resource allocation in both cooperating agencies.

The strategies described next reflect contractual arrangements between the school district and private and public service providers. Contractual arrangements differ from other strategies which use external resources because the cooperation and mutuality which typify the others is not present as part of the agreement. Strategies which incorporate informal or formal cooperative arrangements maximize the effectiveness of existing resources. Contractual arrangements are outright purchases of services; cooperative planning between school districts and contracting service providers is limited to agreeing on extent of service and cost of service.

For the school district, contracting can be an extremely effective means of acquiring necessary services for handicapped children in the district. Contracting for services makes use of externally available resources, and frees the district from start-up costs which can greatly increase the associated service costs. Contracted services fall into the following categories: intermittent or irregularly scheduled services, such as medical, psychological, or physical evaluation and assessments; services to small numbers of students, such as occupational or physical therapy; and services requiring specialized equipment, knowledge, or skills, such as psychiatric counseling. Contracts are practical alternatives for ensuring that the needs of students are met in the most economical and effective manner. Although the per pupil costs are high, the district does not need to invest in supportive equipment or facilities or make long term personnel commitments. In allocating resources, contractual arrangements should be considered along with interagency agreements as methods of ensuring that appropriate services are provided at reasonable costs.

The three strategies presented in this section illustrate a sample of representative approaches to solving service delivery problems. Since districts have more experience in the area of contractual arrangements than with other areas, this section only briefly highlights a few strategies.

Contracts for Referral Information

In many large metropolitan areas that possess a variety of public and private agencies and organizations that are potential service providers, it may be hard to identify the appropriate service provider for the unique needs of the individual. However, the task of organizing, filing, and maintaining a list of service providers would be costly. When one considers the use which would be made of such a resource file, it seems inappropriate for school districts to bear that cost.

A much more practical alternative is to use a private referral service to locate appropriate services. Private referral services sell resource listings to a variety of consumers, thus recovering the costs necessary to develop and maintain the bank. Such services save school districts the costs associated with maintaining a similar system. Use of a referral service enables a school district to identify a greater number of agencies which may be used, through contracts, interagency agreements, or other means, to meet the unique needs of each child.

The referral service described here was used in Galveston, Texas. It maintains a data bank on 1,500 public and private agencies and organizations, as well as files on individuals in child-centered fields. The information contained in the files allows a client to determine the relevance of a service to his or her needs and identifies the service location and mode.

Volunteers and staff compile and update files through site visits to service providers. Funding for the center comes from a variety of sources, including purchased service contracts. Individuals seeking assistance from the center can obtain three free referrals. Charges for directive consultation and other services are based on a sliding scale.

Contracts with referral agencies can facilitate quick and individualized screening of service providers, enabling the vast resources of the community to be brought to bear on the unique problems of each individual child. Only when a variety of service options are examined can the school district ensure that all of a child's special and related service needs are met in the least restrictive environment.

Contracts for Early Childhood Education

Under Public Law 94-142, each state and local education agency must provide a free, appropriate public education to all handicapped children ages 3 through 21 with the exception that for children 3 through 5 and 18 through 21, the requirement does not apply if it is inconsistent with state law or practice or the order of any court (34 CFR §300a.122).

Because many school systems do not possess either the experience or the authority to work with preschool youngsters, this mandate poses an interesting dilemma. Since establishing their own programs would not be cost effective, a number of school districts contract with private nursery schools to provide the mandated services. Placement of handicapped children in local private nursery schools provides the children with group experiences, exposure to nonhandicapped children, and training which will facilitate entry into kindergarten.

In Arlington, Massachusetts, private nursery schools are used and an early childhood coordinator employed by the district works with the directors of the private nursery schools to enable them to effectively serve children with special needs. This individual, in addition to providing technical assistance, has helped to form an Early Childhood Association, and has assisted in fostering more communication among private nursery school directors.

Although this strategy is a contractual arrangement, it also incorporates a cooperative effort on the part of the school district and private nursery schools. It works to the benefit of both. The costs associated with establishing a new program are saved and the handicapped students are educated alongside nonhandicapped children. The various private nursery schools gain from the liaison and support provided by the district's early childhood coordinator. Indeed, their ability to effectively meet the special needs of handicapped children would not be successful without the assistance and support provided by this individual, who is a key to the success of the strategy.

Contracts for Mental Health Services

A strategy described earlier in this chapter involved a cooperative effort between the school district and community-run mental health agency. A different approach taken in Milford, Massachusetts, was to contract for mental health services. The Milford School District found it advantageous to contract for services since the district would then only need to pay for the actual hours of service used. The overhead costs were absorbed by the mental health agency or prorated and figured into the hourly figure. Either method resulted in monetary savings for the district.

The actual contract is between the school district and two mental health agencies. One, a private agency, provides services to students with medical insurance. For other students, the school district has a contract with a public mental health agency which obtains Medicaid funds. Those costs not covered by either private medical insurances or Medicaid are paid by the school district, using other insurance benefits, or federal, state, or local funds.

Unlike the cooperative effort that was undertaken in Arlington, the services provided in Milford are limited to the provision of direct services to the student or to the parents and, to a limited extent, to faculty members. Although this strategy has provided a cost-effective mechanism for providing mental health services to students, some concerns have been raised. Staff from the two mental health agencies provide the service in the school buildings, yet their presence is not completely understood or accepted by members of the school faculty. Furthermore, there are problems associated with pulling students out of scheduled classes for once-weekly activities. It is difficult for the teacher to accept when this is done by another faculty member; it is more difficult still when it is done by an "outsider" who has not established credibility or rapport with the faculty.

From the therapists' point of view, the lack of an adequate physical setting in which to conduct individual and group counseling and the lack of a storage area for supplies is a nuisance. The contractual nature of the relationship may actually hinder the development of solutions to problems like these. Although these problems exist, they are not unsolvable. They should be considered, however, in the implementation of this strategy.

Summary: Contractual Arrangements

Contracts for the delivery of services to handicapped children enable greater flexibility within the school district, especially when the services to be provided involve low incidence populations or unique needs. The strategies presented in this section were selected to illustrate ways to use contractual arrangements in order to provide more flexibility to districts. Internal delivery systems for such services require a minimum number of students in order to be economical. Contracts cover only the actual hours of service provided and a prorated share of the overhead costs. Since the establishment of internal programs using internal resources often restricts the flexibility of the school district to meet varied needs in a variety of settings, the use of contracts is not a statement of incompetence on the part of the district, but rather an action that displays organized, comprehensive, and efficient service delivery.

Furthermore, there are circumstances in which contractual arrangements are the most cost-effective use of available resources. For example, to hire a full time nurse to monitor the severe medical needs of a single handicapped child would be ineffective and inefficient.

The federal mandate for meeting the unique needs of handicapped children in the lease restrictive environment requires, above all, service delivery flexibility on the part of the school district. The individual needs of the child change as he or she progresses through the school system; new children may possess vastly different needs. The "work" costs associated with establishing full and comprehensive internal delivery systems must be weighed against program flexibility. Federal legislation has assisted in suggesting a comprehensive array of service options which must be available for children. Now school administrators must continue to seek effective, economically balanced ways to provide quality educational programs in least restrictive environments for all students.

CONCLUSION

Within the past decade, observers of the educational process have witnessed a dramatic change in the tenor of community involvement in the schools. Parents and others in the community have come to be regarded by school administrators as a viable asset with tremendous potential. Community groups have come to be regarded as knowledgeable partners in the administrator's efforts to assist in the development of the whole child. This chapter highlighted strategy prototypes which suggest ways in which community members and agencies can be integrated in the educational process of providing a free, appropriate education to students in the least restrictive environment.

The strategies presented in the chapter also illustrate a variety of options that assist school administrators in providing special education and related services to meet the unique needs of individual students. Most of these strategies represented attempts to supplement or extend existing internal resources without adding to costs. Supplemental resources to provide a wide range of services are available to school districts. The responsibility to provide experiences that facilitate growth of the handicapped individual cannot rest solely with the educational system since related service needs transcend the traditional boundaries of the educational system. The needs of handicapped children cannot be adequately met by the sole use of parochial strategies that resolve service delivery problems through internal resource management.

As mentioned earlier, these three categories of community involvement strategies and resources, interagency agreements, and contractual arrangements may be differentiated on several factors. First, the time needed to establish the relationship between the LEA and the community group varies. Relationships may be easily and quickly formed in the case of utilizing community resources and even with contractual arrangements since these are formed legally to meet clear-cut, mutual service needs. However, building an interagency agreement with another service group may emerge only over time after professionals have served together informally, performing other, related functions. The area of professional turf is also a major consideration to be resolved in forming interagency agreements.

Second, the amount of time required for planning these three strategy types must be considered. While community resource strategies may be quickly planned, interagency agreements and, particularly, contractual arrangements require much more formal planning time and development of concise statements of their mutual responsibilities. Without these statements, even the best of relationships may be impaired in efforts to provide effective, efficient service.

Third, the extent of commitment required by parties to the agreement must be considered. While all strategy types require a basic commitment to provide services to students in most appropriate, least restrictive environments, the formality of the commitment varies according to the strategy type. Community resources require informal, mutually satisfactory relationships between the LEA and a community group, while interagency agreements require a more formal delineation of duties and responsibilities needed to provide coordinated services. Contractual arrangements, as legal documents, represent a high degree of formality in solidifying the LEA-community organization relationship.

Fourth, the duration of services must be considered. This factor is probably most variable among community resource strategies which are quickly started and minimally funded. These strategies have required only small amounts of district time and effort; therefore, they may be quickly altered or adapted in other ways to better meet changing district needs. Since community resource strategies are also informal arrangements, they may have been planned for only short periods of time and may be supported further and more formally if they assist administrators to provide more appropriate services. Both interagency agreements and contractual arrangements, as formal strategies, are developed over more lengthy periods of time. District commitment may be higher in terms of fiscal support and resources committed to strategy planning, implementation, and maintenance; therefore, these may be regarded as more long-term types of strategies.

Finally, strategy categories may be differentiated by the flexibility or latitude that exists in the agreement. Typically, the less formal the arrangement, the greater degree of flexibility which is available to alter or redesign the strategy. For example, community resource strategies (informal) may be easily rearranged while contractual arrangements (formal) may be changed only by redrawing the legal contract.

Selecting Strategies to Coordinate Community Resources

Community resource strategies naturally require a coordination of the program within the community. They may require reassignment of some personnel for short or intermittent periods of time to provide ongoing consultation and guidance during the strategy's implementation phase. For example, consultants may be needed to assist periodically on specific projects. Community resource strategies are also characterized by the minimal levels of funding which are needed during development and implementation, and for their quick start-up time.

There are several district characteristics which need to be considered when implementing community resource strategies. These strategies do not typically require coordination with state or intermediate education units. They may be used either in large, complex districts or within smaller districts with direct administrative relationships among administrators. Community resource strategies are recommended if the district is experiencing a personnel shortage in specific areas of concern. A few require the allocation of building space, while most may be easily implemented in geographically dispersed areas.

Selecting Strategies to Implement Interagency Agreements

In contrast, interagency agreement strategies are characterized by a greater degree of coordination not only within the community, but also within school buildings. Most interagency agreement strategies require intensive staff development for participating personnel as well as the employment of new personnel. Substantial funds are usually needed to implement these strategies. They also require lengthy periods for development and/or implementation.

District concerns are multiple in the selection of interagency agreement strategies for implementation. While these strategies may be implemented in the same administrative structures as the community resource strategies, suitability of program location (i.e., urban or rural area) is not a concern since agreements may be formed among groups in any area where mutual service needs are being met. Most interagency strategies require some building space so that outside service providers may have space to work when at the LEA. Personnel needs in interagency agreements are specific to each individual strategy.

Selecting Strategies to Facilitate Contractual Arrangements

The most formal type of community involvement strategy, contractual arrangements, are characterized by the minimal degree of change which they require of the LEA. They usually require no change in the job responsibilities of staff and no intensive staff development for persons involved in these activities; however, they do require continuous, ongoing consultation activities. While the contractual arrangements reported in this chapter were implemented with minimal funds, the amount of time for strategy development, implementation, and maintenance is much more than is required by the previous two strategy types.

Contractual arrangements may be useful to districts which are experiencing a shortage of personnel or in urban or small areas where program sites are separated by large distances. However, they are not generally well-adapted in districts with limited building space since most require rooms for part-time services provided by consultant or itinerant personnel. Contractual arrangements may be used regardless of the specific administrative structure of the individual district as long as the program coordination function is assumed by a clearly delineated group.

Concluding Comments

Many problems face educators in their efforts to educate students in appropriate educational environments, even when a variety of means of obtaining supplemental resources is considered. Roles and responsibilities among community service providers still remain clouded and unclear. The flexibility of school districts to utilize certain resources is influenced by state or federal regulations and legislation. Although the educational system has been made responsible for advising or remediating many problems outside its traditional realm, creative strategies for employing community-wide resources are sometimes viewed with skepticism. Therefore, a comprehensive approach is necessary to organizing and using available resources for identified needs.

The schools should be the vehicle for ensuring that the resources of the community are brought to bear on the needs of the handicapped child, but they need not be the only vehicle for providing these services. It is hoped that the strategies provided in this chapter will cause administrators to question the effectiveness of establishing a program using school system resources when services could be better provided through cooperative efforts or through contractual arrangements.

3

Communication

SHARON L. RAIMONDI

An effective communication system among all components of the educational system can facilitate the process of educating handicapped children in least restrictive environments. Special educators are realizing that they no longer belong in a separate world, isolated from regular education, but are an integral part of the educational system. It is the responsibility of both regular and special education administrators to establish an effective communication system, thus creating one mode to assist in the delivery of an appropriate education for all children.

Communication occurs naturally within the educational setting among all individuals including administrators, teachers, parents, students, secretaries, custodial staff, and the multitude of people who come in contact with the schools daily. However, LEA administrators have pointed out an increasing need for better communication to accompany their efforts to integrate handicapped students.

These efforts have affected educational communications in many ways. Special education has become the focus of increased public attention, controversy, and concern within communities. This attention reflects an increasing desire on the part of the community members to know what is going on in their schools. Thus, school communications with the community are important in the successful provision of a free, appropriate public education for handicapped students.

Second, the increased workload of central office administrators has in many cases forced them to reduce their direct contact with the schools. Similarly, principals have less opportunity for interaction with building level staff. At the same time, however, their need for strong communication has increased, since administrative and planning functions have become more complex and a greater number of students with a wider range of educational needs have entered the school system.

Third, an appropriate education within the least restrictive environment means greater involvement in the regular class for many students. Thus, regular and special educators must increase their interaction. As more handicapped students enter regular classes, special and regular teachers will more often be providing instruction to the same students. In addition, larger portions of their respective areas of expertise will need to be shared.

Finally, the integration of handicapped students calls for maximizing their opportunity to interact with their nonhandicapped peers. Concern for the socialization of handicapped students as well as for implementing the intent of the laws leads to the recognition that student-to-student communication should also be facilitated. Such communication can help to ease the transition of handicapped students from segregated settings to regular classes and discourage their social isolation.

Thus, there is a need to evaluate existing structures and redefine, restructure, or develop stronger communication between regular education, special education, and the community. A strong communication system is necessary to assist in the development and maintenance of the major changes that have been made in the educational system.

Target audiences for school communications may be viewed as comprising an internal public and external public. The external public includes the general community and parents. While there are specific strategies to enhance school communications with each of these groups, there are also strategies which may be effective with both.

The internal public consists of administrators, staff, and students. Numerous people who are attached to the internal system such as secretaries, custodial staff, or other school-related personnel may also be included in this group. By defining the internal public in this manner, communication regarding special education is viewed not only as a concern of the special education administrator, but also as a concern of the regular education administrator. With so many members of the internal public of the schools involved in the education of a student, it is necessary for an administrator to have available a number of strategies that will keep him or her in touch with their activities and facilitate their intercommunication. This is particularly true when special education is perceived as an integrated entity within education.

This chapter has five parts. The first two describe strategies for strengthening communication between the school system and the external public—the community and parents. Then communication within and between internal components of the educational system is discussed, including communication between administrators and school staff, communication among staff within a school building, and finally, communication among students.

THE EXTERNAL PUBLIC

With policies toward the education of handicapped children changing so rapidly, the community has become increasingly concerned about the implications for all education. The community can be a source of financial and political support for change within the school system. In addition, communications with the community in general also reach parents, who are the primary subgroup of concern within the external public. Many of the following strategies are useful in strengthening communications with the community in general, including parents. These strategies are presented in the first of the following two sections. Strategies to communicate directly with parents are then presented.

Strengthening Communication with the Community

In order to maintain the support of their communities, local educational agencies must ensure that information about educational policies, activities, and achievements is exchanged in a strong, interactive system of communication. In this section, three strategies that enhance school communications with the community are presented. The first two strategies provide opportunities for interaction with community members and the third provides information about educational policies and activities through public information media.

Offering a Candidates' Night for Potential School Board Members

School boards, as a result of increased taxpayer pressure, have begun to take a more critical look not only at budgets and programs, but also at regular and special education operations. In such an environment, it is important that special interest groups such as parents, teachers, and friends of handicapped children know the views and thoughts of school board candidates prior to the election. It is also important that candidates receive information about programs and information about the thoughts, views, and feelings of the special interest groups. An opportunity for such two-way communication was provided by the strategy investigated in Santa Monica, California.

Candidates for the school board election were invited to a special candidates' night meeting sponsored by the district advisory committee for special education. Each candidate was sent a packet of information on the special education program and was invited to visit special education classes. At the meeting, candidates made short presentations expressing their views on special education and generally explained why the parents, teachers, and friends of handicapped children in attendance should vote for them. Following the presentation, questions from the audience were answered and then all in attendance had the opportunity to interact informally. The event was well-publicized and one of the largest audiences for any gathering of this type was assembled to hear the candidates.

Both candidates and constituents benefited from the evening's activities. Candidates had the opportunity to explain their positions on special education and to learn of the concerns, priorities, and thoughts of parents, teachers, and friends of handicapped students regarding the district's special education program. Members of this special interest group had the opportunity to listen to candidates' positions on special education and to share their opinions with the candidates. Such two-way communication ensures that decisions (electoral and programmatic) are based on high quality information and awareness of the facts.

Formulating a Community Advisory Committee

The California Master Plan mandates the establishment of Community Advisory Committees (CAC). The CAC's primary function is to advise California's responsible local agencies in the development and implementation of the Master Plan. The CAC also aids in the evaluation of the district's program of instruction. Although this is a state-wide strategy, the following account describes the Community Advisory Committee of the Santa Monica Schools.

Communication is the essential function of the CAC. Regular monthly meetings provide time for members to interact with school personnel and to work on projects. In addition to candidates' night, three special open meetings are organized by the CAC each year; these meetings feature stimulating speakers who address concerns common to parents, educators, and interested citizens regarding topics in special education. Communication is also encouraged by regular newsletters that are written and disseminated under the direction of CAC. In addition, a parents' handbook was written and printed through funding made available under the Master Plan. These kinds of proactive interchanges among people facilitate the development of positive attitudes and a sense of working together.

A major distinction between the Community Advisory Committee and previous parent advocacy groups is that, while there is an emphasis placed on parental involvement (parents comprise at least 60% of the membership), there is also a concerted effort to involve the entire community. When the CAC was first being formed, one concern was to ensure that the group was not viewed as a rival by local PTA organizations. For this reason, all local PTA presidents were asked to select a representative to serve on the CAC. Many local PTAs now have a PTA Special Education Chairperson who serves on the CAC.

Another consideration when establishing the CAC is the strength of the initial leadership. When an organization is developing, strong leadership is essential. If the influence of the organization is to grow and the organization is to gain the respect and support of the broader community, it must have credibility. An organization without a history acquires its credibility and direction from the strength and personality of the leader.

It is also important to build pride in membership among group members and to establish a sense of group credibility. One of the best ways to accomplish this is to focus the energy and enthusiasm of the members on projects which are not only meaningful but which also produce tangible products such as the newsletters and parents' handbook developed by the group described here. This helps the members of the group to develop a sense of group identity and group pride which increases their willingness to remain involved and to continue to work with school personnel, an important consideration in volunteer activities. For a group like the CAC to be effective, its members must work as a team toward group goals rather than following individual agendas.

As a result of the CAC, parents have a vehicle to communicate their concerns and obtain support. A network has been established that links parents, educators, administrators, and community members through communication and interaction. Involvement with school personnel is increased and educational services and programs are improved.

Using the Public Media

Humboldt-Del Norte School District of California often uses public media to provide information to citizens about educational activities. Newspapers and local news programs on television and radio are used. To maintain good relationships with media personnel, school district representatives make every effort to inform the public of events within the school district, emphasizing special education in particular. Establishment and maintenance of a good relationship with media representatives is important to the ability to get coverage.

Facilitating Communication with Parents

Parents are the primary subgroup of concern within the external public. In the past, schools and parents of handicapped students were often in adversary positions. Many educators were resented for designing educational programs with minimal parental input. In addition, schools working under budgetary constraints found they could not operate enough programs and classes. Parents who were desperate for help began demanding programs for their children, but because they were not involved in the process or well-informed regarding external constraints, they become frustrated and angry. At the very least, parents need to be kept well-informed of their child's progress. However, they should also be made aware of their child's educational milieu and the various forces acting upon it. In order to develop such awareness they should be involved in activities that affect their child's education. Parents who are left without support and without involvement are a wasted resource and potential adversaries.

Parents must feel welcome and at ease if they are to assist in planning their child's education. However, although they are partners in this process, parents rarely have the opportunity to acquire new educational skills or expand their knowledge of educational techniques. Without strong communication, neither parents nor educational personnel can develop empathy toward the roles and responsibilities of the other. Parental understanding of the impact of new legislation on the education of both handicapped and nonhandicapped children needs to be fostered so that myths and misunderstandings can be clarified. Strategies that strengthen community interaction also strengthen interaction with parents, since they are often the most interested members of the community.

Encouraging Parental Involvement in In-service Activities

Educational literature often cites the important role played by parents in the educational process. However, a parent rarely has the opportunity to acquire new knowledge or skills in specific educational techniques. Also, because of different orientations toward the child, few parents or teachers possess a thorough understanding of each other's role and responsibilities. The Lynnfield School District in Massachusetts, recognizing the need for parents and community members to understand the impact of recent special educational legislation on educational programs, has extended to parents the opportunity to participate in in-service programs.

The Lynnfield School District provides in-service activities that are both district-wide and building oriented. When facilities and content allow, parents are invited to attend in-service sessions. Information regarding these activities is published in the community newspaper and notices encouraging parents to attend are sent home with the children. When all parents cannot be accommodated, representatives from the parent organization are invited to attend. The names of those representatives are published along with the notice of the in-service activity to enable parents and other interested community members to learn about the activities.

The district's special education in-service training programs emphasize identification and accommodation of student learning styles. Through these activities, teachers of nonhandicapped children have come to recognize that all children have different learning styles and that the learning styles of handicapped children represent a different degree or intensity of style. This basic in-service philosophy is also appropriate for parents.

A strategy to provide an opportunity for parents to become involved in in-service activities does not require additional resources. Typically, few parents are able to attend, but those who do respond favorably to the strategy. The school's acceptance of parents as partners in the educational process and the communication channels that are opened help to strengthen the bond between home and school. Parents feel welcome at the school and gain a better understanding of the teacher's role and perspective while sharing their perceptions. With this added understanding, teachers and parents are better able to work together to ensure continuity and consistency. Even parents who have never attended in-service sessions sense the openness and sincerity that is behind the strategy and are also able to gain information from parent representatives.

Summary: The External Public

Efforts to strengthen interaction between communities and their educational systems can produce a variety of benefits. As described in Chapter 2, increased community interaction can help to provide additional resources to the educational system, as well as increasing political support for educational policies and activities.

Without strong communications, such support may be difficult to obtain. Community members must be provided information about changing educational activities, either through public information media or through direct interaction with the educational system. As taxpayers, citizens should be encouraged to contribute their thoughts and ideas to educational planning with their communities. The strategies of the previous chapters as well as those described here provide administrators with techniques for encouraging interactions which can provide valuable information to the school system and at the same time can provide citizens with the knowledge they need in order to understand and support educational activities.

As members of the community, as partners in the educational process, and as a valuable resource to schools, parents are the primary group of concern within the external public. Strategies which strengthen communication with the community also facilitate information with parents, so administrators who wish to strengthen communication with parents should consider the strategies targeted at the community at large as well as those designed specifically to reach parents.

THE INTERNAL PUBLIC

As more handicapped children are educated in less restrictive settings, the growing need for more effective communication between regular and special education becomes apparent. The internal component of a school system is comprised of many subcomponents, including, but not limited to, administrators, teachers, and students. With so many members of the internal public of the schools involved in the education of a student, it is necessary for an administrator to have available a number of strategies that will facilitate the communication process.

Communication strategies are often viewed in terms of their effectiveness in disseminating information downward through the administrative hierarchy; however, the importance of strategies which assist administrators in the collection of information from teachers, support staff, community members, and parents should also be emphasized. Strategies to obtain necessary information from diverse audiences are needed to facilitate efforts to provide appropriate services to students in least restrictive settings. Such strategies provide necessary information for planning, budgeting, and providing educational programming. Strategies which represent ways for administrators to secure information for these purposes are presented in this section.

Reinforcing Communication Between Administrators and School Personnel

Since school districts are typically arranged in a hierarchical fashion with some administrators housed in a central office while other administrators and personnel are located at the local building level, the direct exchange of information on the functioning of the schools is often limited.

One of the uses for information from the school building level is planning. Various strategies described in previous chapters strengthen administrators' communication with the schools in regard to their planning and evaluation responsibilities. These include the Program Implementation Review (PIR) discussed in Chapter 1, a survey originally used in Humboldt-Del Norte, California, to monitor compliance with the California Master Plan. Later, the PIR evolved into a communications tool for exchange of information covering a broader range of topics, including school needs and program status and quality.

Administrators also need some mechanism through which to supply specific policy and program information to the schools. Except for the special education teacher, there is often no one at the building level with expertise to answer the daily questions concerning special education policy or to deal with problems as they arise. As more handicapped students are educated with their nonhandicapped peers, regular education teachers and principals have an increased need to communicate with the administrative staff of special education.

Because it is not always physically possible for the special education director to visit each building daily, some districts have developed formal communication links between the special education administrator and the schools. Personnel roles have either been created or modified to provide this link in some districts. Several of these roles were described in other chapters. Special education personnel, such as liaisons, area representatives, consultants, facilitators, and evaluation team chairpersons, all provide a direct line of communication between building staff and special and/or regular education administrators.

The discussions in this section illustrate additional strategies to improve communication between administrators and school building personnel. In addition to a newsletter which provides information from administrators to district staff, several strategies illustrate ways to gather information from the building level for administrative use. These strategies range from simple surveys that collect information on broad areas through alert sheets and needs assessments that bring administrative attention to particular problems or needs, to surveys and questionnaires accompanied by interviews which both collect broad information on school functioning and allow in-depth, verbal information on specific topics of interest or concern. The strategies of this section illustrate this continuum of information gathering techniques.

Distributing a School-Wide Newsletter

St. Paul, Minnesota, not unlike other districts, distributes a monthly newsletter to special education teachers and other staff. This newsletter is unique, however, because it is written by the assistant superintendents of elementary and secondary education and the special education director in joint collaboration.

This strategy has produced multiple benefits. Not only does the newsletter communicate with staff within the district, but it also stimulates communication among its authors, focusing their attention on the concerns and issues of special education. Thus, the newsletter has resulted in an improved understanding of special education by elementary and secondary assistant superintendents and a reciprocal understanding of elementary and secondary education by the special education director.

Employing a Questionnaire to Assess Needs

A form called the In-Service Training Interest Inventory is used in Contra Costa, California, to "facilitate communication, plan and deliver inservice programs, and develop and coordinate resources (such as people and materials), to provide an ongoing staff development program." Although this inventory is used for gathering information on staff development in Contra Costa, similarly structured inventories may be developed for gathering information on other broad areas of interest.

Using the form, regular educators are asked to specify their preferred topics. Twenty-one possible topics are offered. The respondents are asked to choose and rank the three items which represent their highest interest and state their preferred delivery modes (e.g., workshop or presentation). These are reported on a summary chart like the one presented in Figure 1. The information collected from regular educators is then summarized by the resource specialist in each school, and a copy is sent to the staff development specialist, who uses it to plan in-service training activities. Similar inventories could be used to assess needs in a variety of areas. The selection and ranking techniques used in this inventory assure that a realistic array of responses is received, and the summary chart provided by the respondent reduces the workload of those who analyze the data.

FIGURE 1
Example of a Summary Chart

Preferred Topics	Item Number	Implementation Code
First Choice	16	V
Second Choice		
Third Choice		

Developing a Problem Alert Sheet

Rural districts often have problems maintaining effective ongoing communication systems. The special education division of Humboldt-Del Norte, a large, rural school district, instituted an informal communication mechanism several years ago to solve this problem. The purpose of the strategy is to provide a system whereby any person in any school could contact the central office for assistance with the education of handicapped students and be assured of a timely response.

Problem alert sheets are distributed to all schools. They provide space for the following information: (a) a description of the problem, (b) suggested solutions, (c) action taken, (d) names and titles of persons completing the form, and (e) date completed and received at the central office. After forms are completed, they are returned to the assistant director of special education, who reviews requests and routes them to the appropriate staff member. In this way, requests for assistance are received and acted on quickly, usually within a week. A key factor in the success of this process is the prompt and appropriate response by the administrative staff.

In addition to providing an effective communication mechanism between the central office and the field, the problem alert sheets provide an on-going source of information. Peak request periods for overtime work are identified and staff needs are anticipated. Requests from the field allow staff to spot trends and recurring problems and modify procedures such as forms, reports, and data collection requirements. For example, when speech therapists complained that the district IEP format did not correspond to their departmental requirements, a problem alert sheet was used to highlight the problem; an immediate positive response from central office staff resulted in the modification of the IEP form.

Assessing Needs by Analyzing Assistance Requests

The Contra Costa staff development specialist also provides teachers with another means to express their needs. This is the Self-Select Assistance Menu (SAM). Copies of a SAM, which lists 21 potential assistance areas, are provided to each instructor. Topics may be selected at any time and assistance is provided by either the building-level resource specialist or the staff development department.

This form provides instructional staff with a method for assessing their needs on a continual basis and obtaining immediate assistance. In that sense, this strategy is similar to the problem alert sheet described earlier. Also like the problem alert sheet, it allows trends to be analyzed. However, with the use of this strategy, teachers can request assistance without labeling their assistance needs as problems.

Using Questionnaires and Interviews to Obtain Information

In California, the San Juan Unified School District conducts a yearly evaluation of their special education program. The evaluation is designed to provide the state education agency with required data as well as to give the district information needed to assist in annual planning efforts. In developing the evaluation instrument, the school district identified the following four areas: (a) locating and serving all students with exceptional needs, (b) improving instruction and services. (c) increasing teacher and parent satisfaction and (d) maintaining and improving the program.

Graduate students from a local college are trained to conduct the interviews. Several additional sources of data are used for the evaluation, including testing information from teacher and student files, student reports, on-site evaluation, face-to-face interviews, phone surveys, studies of IEPs, and student observations. Additional information is gleaned throughout the year from numerous other sources.

The face-to-face interviews are conducted with regular and special education students, administrators, teachers, and school assessment teams. A sample of 140 students is interviewed yearly. The sample includes three Resource Specialist Program students, three Learning Development Class students, and three regular class students in each of the district's 16 schools. Interviews are scheduled and conducted at each school. The survey assesses student attitudes toward school, study, other students, and self. There are three levels of survey forms for use with primary, middle, and secondary school students. Additional surveys gather information from parents and survey special education staff. A comprehensive report on the interviews with staff and students is given to the special education program supervisors, specialists, and resource teachers at the end of the school year.

This strategy can be used to provide administrators and other staff members with summary information on the pulse of the schools. Much of the information provided through this far-reaching technique would be difficult to obtain if less thorough methods were utilized. For example, information on student and parent attitudes is not only included, but is also displayed against the context of other school and district variables. Although this technique is more complex than the other strategies which communicate building-level information to administrators, it is also more thorough and can provide administrators with a composite picture of educational life in the schools and in the district.

Promoting Communication Between Special and Regular Education Teachers

Interpersonal and small group communication between regular and special educators is necessary to facilitate the delivery of services to handicapped students. As the number of handicapped children simultaneously assigned to regular and special education teachers increases, so does the need for communication between regular and special educators.

The process of developing a handicapped child's individual educational plan requires a concerted effort by all involved parties. To ensure that each child receives an appropriate and consistent program, it is critical that open lines of communication are established among all parties at the local building level and that these lines of communication continue through the school year. Administrators must establish a support system to encourage such communication.

Such support and communication can be established in a variety of ways. All of the prereferral strategies described in Chapter 2, for example, provide support for the regular education teacher and foster communication between regular and special education teachers and other staff, as well. These include child study teams, school guidance committees, building screening committees, and learning teams. Of these prereferral teams, the child study teams provide regular education teachers with more knowledge of special education techniques, since they include some training. The individual prereferral strategy described in Chapter 2, the generic teacher of Massachusetts, provides regular teachers with direct, one-to-one support.

Team teaching is an excellent mechanism for promoting communication between special education and regular teachers, as is dual certification for regular educators. These strategies are described in Chapter 4, Personnel Utilization. Two additional strategies are described below.

Using a Written Report to Communicate Daily Student Progress

In an attempt to improve communications between regular education and special education teachers, regular education teachers are provided a form by which to communicate each student's progress to the special education teacher on a daily basis. The form also serves as a modifier of students' behavior since it may be incorporated into a behavior management plan. Feeling a need to coordinate the activities of all regular teachers involved with one handicapped student, the resource teachers implemented this strategy.

Each student is responsible for presenting his or her form to the regular education teachers, who then mark the appropriate boxes. When the student reports to the resource room, the card is reviewed with the student by the resource teacher. When the resource teacher feels that communication has been established and daily feedback is not required, the forms are used once a week instead of daily. Such a system provides a means for regular and special educators to establish interpersonal communication.

Scheduling Horizontal Basic Classes

Another strategy to promote appropriate instruction of elementary students and to facilitate communication between special and regular education teachers is found in Dallas, Texas. In the district, a horizontal grouping procedure for the basic elementary subjects is used. The program is scheduled so that all children within a specific grade receive reading and math instruction at the same time. Thus, if a student needs to be moved upward to a higher reading or math class within the same grade (but with a different teacher), the move is easily made. Conversely, when a student needs more intensive efforts in reading or math, he or she may be moved to the more appropriate reading or math group. Scheduling basic classes at the same time across grades facilitates teacher planning for individualized instruction. Scheduling basic classes to facilitate communication among teachers also has the additional benefit of promoting social interaction among handicapped and nonhandicapped students. An additional strategy to encourage communication among students is presented below.

Facilitating Communication with Students

In order to truly integrate handicapped students, administrators must provide them with maximum opportunity to interact with their nonhandicapped peers and to have similar school experiences. The strategy presented in this section facilitates student-to-student interaction by locating programs for handicapped students in close physical proximity to regular classes, thus allowing students an opportunity to interact.

Locating Special Education Programs in Appropriate Settings

Communication among all students can be promoted by locating special programs in close proximity to regular classes. In Stanislaus, California, the decision was made to locate the communicatively handicapped (CH) and orthopedically handicapped (OH) programs in two open-space schools which were to be constructed in the district.

The schools were to provide open space settings with central cores to accommodate relocation or portable buildings already owned by the district. The CH classes were housed in the center of the school in order to enhance the opportunities of CH children to have special contact with other students.

The new buildings allowed principals and staff to be selected specifically for the new programs. Intensive in-service training programs were offered, including instruction in signing for teachers and students. In turn, the principal and staff worked with parents of CH and regular students in planning for the new school.

The principal, two special education teachers and two unit leaders were the primary persons to implement the program. Unit leaders were regular education teachers who were assigned some supervisory responsibilities for lower and upper elementary units. The unit leaders worked closely with principals and regular and special teachers to facilitate integration. They met regularly with teachers in their unit and planned with CH teachers for mainstreaming. Unit leaders indicated that since the principal encouraged their leadership role, teachers felt willing to discuss problems with them.

Integration efforts were planned for each child in the program. The in-service support to teachers increased teachers' confidence in their ability to work with CH children. Although this strategy was used in a new building in Stanislaus, its basic focus—housing special and regular programs in the same building and making provision for communication among students—is a relevant consideration whenever students are relocated.

Summary: The Internal Public

It is crucial to strengthen communications between schools and central administration at a time when changes in school operations, programs, and needs are occurring in conjunction with changes in administrative responsibility.

Chapter 1 presented strategies that use coordinative personnel to assist in communicating and decentralizing other administrative responsibilities. The strategies presented in this section represent additional techniques to convey specific policy and program information to the schools and to provide administrators with information needed for planning and evaluation.

However, the success of a district's program for the education of handicapped children is often dependent on the attitudes of the entire school staff. Regular and special educators need to have open lines of communication which encourage daily interaction. As co-workers, educators must approach each problem as a joint effort in order to find solutions which allow teachers to receive reciprocal support as they work to provide appropriate instruction to all students. When teachers realize that the education of handicapped students must be shared, joint processes can work to benefit all involved persons.

Support systems such as those described in this section should facilitate shared expertise between the merging special and regular education domains by increasing interaction in curriculum development, interpersonal communication among teachers regarding student progress, and scheduling to allow flexibility of student movement between classes. In addition, the increasing involvement of regular education staff in the education of handicapped students makes it important to foster positive relationships between these two very important groups within the internal public. In addition, student-to-student communications should be fostered. Such communication can help to ease the transition of handicapped students entering regular schools and classes and can help to discourage the social isolation of new students.

CONCLUSION

This chapter has emphasized the need for school districts to strengthen communications within and among components of the educational system in response to changes in special education. Many of the strategies described in previous chapters strengthen communication while simultaneously accomplishing some other function. In this chapter, additional strategies to strengthen communication were described. Administrators who wish to strengthen communications with their external public or within their educational systems should consider strategies described in previous chapters as well as those described here.

Strategies for Strengthening Communication with the Community

Given the permeable boundaries of the school with outside organizations as well as the need to coordinate service delivery with and among community groups, ways are needed to ensure a flow of information. Communication will allow community resources to be brought to bear on school related problems and will ensure that community members may serve as valued consultants to school administrators and supporters of school programs and supplies.

Many traditional methods to share information with the community have been used. This section highlighted the use of the public media, the development of a community advisory committee, and the offering of a candidates' night as three strategies administrators are using to promote effective communication with the external public. Both district and strategy characteristics influence the success of these communication strategies.

The communication strategies to use the public media and to formulate a community advisory committee are easily used regardless of the organizational relationship of the LEA to the SEA and/or intermediate units. One could predict that a community advisory committee would be easier to develop in a district that has coordinated regular and special education administrations, although this is not essential for the success of the strategy. All of these community communication strategies could be easily used regardless of personnel availability; however, the community advisory committee's work is greatly facilitated when given the prominence of a special education director's attendance at each committee meeting.

Staff development requirements are not a major factor in strategy selection; while the formation of a community advisory committee requires ongoing consultation with a district liaison, the remaining two strategies require no direct staff development. None of the community communications strategies requires a large amount of funding. The public media strategy may be implemented with minimal or no funds since public information media look for stories of interest to the community; conducting a candidates' night requires no new funds; and the community advisory committee requires only minimal funding for operating expenses and secretarial services. While the public media strategy may be quickly implemented, the development of a community advisory committee and planning a candidates' night require more time for implementation.

Exchanging Information with Parents

If parents are to be partners with school personnel in the educational process, they must be well-informed regarding current developments within the school system as well as within other fields which have impact on the education of handicapped students. While strategies that strengthen communication with the community also strengthen communication with parents, this chapter offered an additional strategy specifically developed to assist schools in exchanging information with parents. This was a means of encouraging parental involvement in in-service activities. While these are not all-encompassing in terms of what administrators can do to facilitate information exchange with parents and the community, they do represent successful attempts to involve parents in an effort to ensure appropriate programming for all students.

The parental involvement in inservice strategy may work more easily where there is a direct link between the SEA and LEA with no intermediate units. Providing in-service to parents requires consideration of space only to the degree that rooms for conducting these activities are of sufficient size to comfortably accommodate all participants. This strategy requires coordination at the community level and at the district level. The provision of inservice activities requires only minimal funds for extra materials and refreshments, and may be quickly implemented.

Reinforcing Communication Between Administrators and School Personnel

The strength of the link between administrative and central office personnel and other school staff provides a direct indication of the sufficiency of established communication channels. As more handicapped students are integrated into regular education environments, a need to reinforce old communication links and to establish new ones has become apparent. In this section, strategies to achieve these goals were presented. These included a newsletter edited by the associate superintendents of elementary and secondary education and the special education director, questionnaires to evaluate special education services, a problem alert sheet for school personnel to use whenever difficulties are encountered, the Self-Assist Menu which provided instructional staff with a method of quickly obtaining support in working with handicapped students, and an in-service interest/training inventory.

The in-service interest/training inventory and the system-wide newsletter are particularly suited for districts which have a shortage of personnel. All of these strategies may be used in urban or small areas. The use of questionnaires is not suited to districts that cover wide geographical areas due to the difficulty of obtaining follow-up interviews. Where building space is limited, the Self-Assist Menu, the inservice inventory, and problem alert sheet are easily used.

All of these strategies need coordination at the district level and the use of questionnaires also requires community coordination since community members are polled. The personnel requirements of these strategies are minimal. The use of questionnaires requires personnel to manage the study and the problem alert sheet and newsletter require minor reassignment of personnel to complete the duties associated with each of these. The others require no additional personnel. All except the newsletter require ongoing consultation. Two strategies, the questionnaires and the newsletter, require substantial funds and planning time. All other strategies may be quickly implemented with minimal funding.

Promotion Communication Between Special and Regular Education Teachers

The importance of a strong relationship between administrators and instructional staff is apparent, but no less important are communication links between special and regular educators. With the expanded domain of special education, regular and special education teachers are now finding that their interests have merged. To support this merger of interests, strong communication strategies are needed. The section on strategies to promote communication between special and regular educators provided examples of ways in which such communication may be fostered.

Two strategies to promote coordination of instructional programs provided by regular and special educators working together were presented. A strategy to communicate student progress among all teachers of an individual student was presented. The second strategy highlighted the need to schedule classes of academic subjects simultaneously in order to facilitate teacher communication and student movement through varying academic levels.

These strategies show similar characteristics regarding ease of implementation across a variety of administrative structures. The availability of personnel is not a major concern in the use of the strategies. While student progress reports may be used without regard to space considerations, coordinating schedules for basic classes may be hampered without adequate instructional space.

Both strategies require coordination at the building level, and the coordination of curriculum may require the reassignment or temporary transfer of present instructional personnel and/or long-term staff development and ongoing consultation. Both initiating a progress report and scheduling instruction to facilitate teacher communication may be quickly implemented with no associated costs.

Facilitating Communication with Students

Student attitudes can be greatly influenced by the level and quality of communication which occurs. In order to provide handicapped students with a smooth social transition from special to regular education environments, strong communication links with students need to be established. In this section, one strategy to facilitate communication with students was presented: locating classes in a manner that promotes the social integration of handicapped students.

It would appear that the strategy to facilitate communication with students would work well in districts where the administrative structure between the central office staff and the local school buildings is direct and where special and regular education administrative structures are integrated. It is also facilitated by environments where there is an abundance of trained instructional personnel.

The program location strategy must be coordinated at the building and district levels. It requires the reassignment or transfer of present personnel, and substantial funds; however, it is also a useful consideration in relocating programs in existing buildings.

Concluding Comments

As the domain of special education expands both within the educational system and throughout the community, the establishment of strong, effective communication links is vital. Efficient communication offers administrators strong support in consolidating the efforts of instructional and support personnel, community members, and advocates for individually determined human development so that appropriate educational programs may be provided to all students attending our nation's schools. Strategies presented within this chapter were designed to provide the school administrator with prototypic examples of methods which may be used to achieve this goal. These strategies should be viewed in conjunction with strategies described in other chapters which also improve communication.

Today, school administrators are facing a great challenge not only to provide comprehensive educational programs, but also to ensure excellence in the services which are offered. While the previous two chapters on administrative systems for service delivery and community involvement and the following two chapters on personnel utilization and staff development present information on the foundation elements of a quality school program, it is the communication strategies which provide the critical links to maintain control and coordination of both the total program and the many subparts contained within it. Administrators striving to provide such a program must review the efficiency of their communication links with both the external public of the community and parents and the internal public of administrators, instructors, and students to determine where new strategies may be most effective. By instituting needed communication innovations with and among vital audiences, school administrators can strengthen the bonds necessary to assure children with special needs a free public education in the least restrictive environment.

4

Personnel Utilization

RONDA C. TALLEY

The inclusion of mildly handicapped students in regular education environments has placed new demands on personnel resources in the public schools. Administrators faced with this challenge of implementing the least restrictive environment mandate have modified service delivery structures in creative and diverse ways that involve new strategies for using personnel. They have redefined the roles of currently employed school personnel and have created new positions which emphasize support, consultation, and coordination. A number of methods to encourage cooperation among regular and special educators have been tested, and innovative strategies for using classroom aides have been observed.

This chapter is divided into two major parts. The first part presents examples of personnel roles that have been created or redefined in order to fill changing needs within service delivery structures. A comparison of the functions assigned to these roles follows.

The second part presents team teaching strategies and innovative strategies for using paraprofessionals. Since each of these strategies was developed to address a single concern or perform a particular function, the conclusion to this part discusses the strategies' adaptability for use in particular school districts.

CREATING OR REDEFINING PERSONNEL ROLES

The personnel roles described in this section were designed by administrators to meet the unique and changing needs of their districts. Efforts to integrate handicapped students have led to requirements for personnel to fill new functions within educational delivery systems. Some of these functions have been to assist administrators in handling an increased workload by decentralizing administrative responsibilities, to help with increased reporting and paperwork requirements, and to provide assistance to regular education staff assigned to handicapped students through consultation, demonstration, and in-service training. In many districts, administrators have chosen to hire new personnel to fill these roles. Other positions have been filled by reassigning and sometimes providing additional training for professionals who were already district employees. The distinction between role creation and role redefinition was discussed by Harris and Bessent in *In-Service Education: A Guide to Better Practice* (1969).

Many considerations enter the decision to redefine the role of a current employee or to establish a new personnel position. It is often easier to redefine an existing position to encompass additional duties or even to execute an entirely different set of responsibilities than to hire a new employee. By ascribing new duties to personnel currently on staff, the administrator is assured that the person filling the new role is already familiar with local policy and the informal structures of the school system. In addition, certain functions may be best filled by someone who is personally known to district or building staff, since bringing in an "outsider" could lead to resentment or could interfere with the performance of the function in some other way. By redefining an existing role, an administrator may be able to take advantage of professional relationships that have already been established. In other situations, it may be more desirable to hire a new employee—the "outsider" status may benefit the role.

An analysis of the newly created and redefined jobs explored by this project showed that some contain primarily administrative functions, some contain technical and instructional assistance functions, and some combine administrative and technical assistance functions. These personnel roles reflect unique district needs and characteristics such as the size of the district and its overall service delivery structure. Considerations such as the assignment of personnel to school buildings or to central or regional administrative offices and associated scheduling concerns are related to both the service delivery structure and the functions encompassed by the personnel role. Such considerations are discussed in the conclusion to this section.

Administrative Positions

The administrative positions described here include coordinative functions such as monitoring the IEP process, facilitating coordination among regular and special education personnel, and providing liaison with central or regional administration. A benefit common to these positions is that they also increase communication. Two administrative positions are presented.

Special Education Area Representatives

When a change in the general administrative structure of a school district that has a dense or geographically disparate population is made, problems may emerge in coordination and communication between regular and special education. Estrangement of these two components may result in the reduction of appropriate services to handicapped students. To avoid such problems, Shawnee Mission, Kansas, has expanded the role of their special education supervisors and program coordinators to include the additional responsibilities of the special education area representative.

In Shawnee Mission, the school district was divided into four areas. To coordinate the delivery of special education services within each area, a special education area representative was appointed. The special education area representative serves several specific functions. The first is to attend area principal meetings in order to present information and to respond to questions or concerns. Second, the representative is responsible for monitoring special education in-service plans and programs. The third function is to be generally responsible for keeping track of current issues and occurrences pertaining to special education within the assigned area.

The position of special education area representative does not represent an additional administrative level; special education program supervisors and coordinators who already had categorical program responsibilities were assigned this responsibility in addition to their regular duties. Direct administrative responsibilities for each of the four areas are still retained by the director of special education. The key role of special education area representatives is to serve as a vital communications link for the director. In this role as communicator, they are supposed to be both visible and accessible to building staff.

In addition to serving as communications link for the director, special education area representatives have provided more accessible and localized lines of communication between regular education and special education. Principals have an accessible contact person when problems, issues or concerns arise. A personally known individual is available to answer questions or to find the answer in a relatively short period of time. Concerns are also routed more quickly and more appropriately by the area representative.

A second important outcome of this role redefinition is that fewer problems arise at area principal meetings. The timely sharing of information and the ability to collect information and get feedback from regular education administrators has enhanced relationships between regular and special education administrators. Principals feel free to call their special education area representatives and receive immediate attention. Likewise, the area special education representative is able to devote more time to schools where the need for information and administrative support is greatest.

Evaluation Team Chairperson

The evaluation team chairperson (ETC) role was established in Natick, Massachusetts, in 1976-1977 to deal with a number of procedural, organizational, and administrative concerns in the district. Currently, 10 evaluation team chairpersons serve the 15 district schools. Some of these positions are part-time. These individuals coordinate full evaluations, partial evaluations and reevaluations for approximately 1,050 students per year.

With the exception of three full-time positions, Natick's ETCs are housed in individual school buildings. They serve as monitors of the evaluation process, assigning responsibility for the completion of various evaluation components to individual study team members. The ETC is responsible for involving parents and junior and senior high school students in the assessment process, and serves as a central contact point for parents throughout the child placement process. At the conclusion of formal schooling, the ETC is also responsible for transferring students with continuing needs into appropriate placements.

There were a number of concerns raised when the ETC role was first established. Administrators, particularly at the building level, were concerned about the creation of a quasiadministrative position. In reality, there is little independent decision making involved in the role, since students' educational plans are arrived at with the parent and other professionals in the evaluation and IEP development process. ETCs coordinate the meetings, document the IEPs and fulfill the Massachusetts requirement that an administrator serve on the evaluation team.

From the ETC perspective, there is the threat of the role becoming a clerical one concerned primarily with the filing of papers and preparation of IEPs. Two factors have lessened this possibility. First, the ETCs are special education professionals, either generic teachers or school social workers. They have a professional, in addition to a coordinating, role and as such, are peers to the other participants in the evaluation process. Second, special education administrators have made it their priority to secure support for these positions so that clerical functions are minimized. It appears that some building principals have also been willing to provide resources to support the work of the ETC and the evaluation team in their building.

Because ETCs are spread among various building sites, there exists a potential for communication breakdown. District administrators have attempted to address this concern by scheduling weekly meetings, usually on Monday morning. These meetings give ETCs a chance to exchange information on specific children moving between buildings or grade levels. Informal contact is also maintained so that the needs of children who are being advanced from elementary to junior high or from junior to senior high have had their needs discussed informally prior to the change. This is a significant concern, since information is needed for reevaluations which occur on the anniversary of the date of initial evaluation, not at the beginning or end of each school year.

Each ETC is assigned to a specific building or buildings in order to develop familiarity with the staff and their needs. Some ETC positions are full time and others are half time, and ETCs are funded totally out of local education agency funds. Funds are available for the special education office to assist part time people with their workload when needed.

The introduction of the ETC role has virtually eliminated a backlog in evaluations. The quality of IEPs has also improved. Parents and principals are pleased. The most significant indication of the success of the role, however, is in the fact that out of 1,050 evaluations performed in the 1978-1979 school year, only 10 were the subject of complaints serious enough to require intervention by the special education administrator.

Providing Technical and Instructional Assistance

The following strategies describe a variety of ways to provide teachers with technical assistance in the areas of classroom modification, instructional techniques and materials, and curriculum development. Since some of the more complex roles require dual certification, a strategy to assist regular educators in obtaining dual certification is described first.

Dual Certification of Regular Educators

One of the simplest forms of role redefinition was encountered in West Columbia, Texas. With this strategy, regular education teachers were asked to assimilate the role of special educators by becoming dually certified in special education.

The process of incorporating this new dimension into the role of the regular educator required the coordination of community and school resources. Since West Columbia is a rural school district with no local college, arrangements were made with two universities to offer special education training. These courses were offered during and after the school day. Courses were held at the school building and tailored to meet the individual needs of the district.

Seventeen of the district's outstanding regular educators were selected to receive a monetary incentive to pursue the program. The use of aides and volunteers provided release time, enabling teachers to attend the classes during school hours. Eventually, classes were opened up for all interested regular educators; ninety took advantage of this opportunity. This retraining of regular educators took place over a two-year period. All teachers paid for the university credit they received.

The dual special education-regular education certification of many of West Columbia's teachers has resulted in a staff more competent to deal with the challenges of instructing all children, including those with special needs. As the focus of education centers more and more on the relevance and appropriateness of instruction in nonstigmatizing environments, models such as this one may be seen more frequently.

Generic Teachers

Generic teachers are trained in special education with emphasis on diagnostic/prescriptive approaches to instructional programming. This role was established in Massachusetts on the principle that the successful integration of mildly handicapped students depends on the availability of a variety of direct and indirect instructional services. The role of the generic teacher provided the coordination through which effective programming could be developed.

Generic teachers are assigned to each school building, usually two to each elementary school. The responsibilities of generic teachers include the provision of direct instructional services to students, consultation with regular educators and other professionals, provision of materials, supplies and information, participation in evaluation assessment activities and team meetings, conferences with parents and the establishment and maintenance of the resource room. Two models of the generic teacher are now used.

Generic teacher model I. One form of Massachusetts' generic teacher model was implemented in Belmont, Massachusetts. In this LEA, regular teachers are certified in special education; however, they function primarily as consultants and secondarily as monitors and coordinators.

Belmont's reasons for creating this model of the generic teacher to provide indirect services were twofold. First, administrators wanted to institute an intermediate step when progressing from a special to a full-time regular education placement. A second and related reason was that Belmont's educators wanted to maintain students in regular classrooms by facilitating successful student performance within that setting.

Generic teachers act as consultants when student performance indicates a need for an environmental or academic change. As a consultant to teachers, the generic teacher provides materials which are compatible with the student's skills and abilities. The generic teacher may offer assistance in the use of these materials or may provide short-term, direct services to the student(s) in the classroom. Demonstration of instructional techniques in the class is one other consultative service offered to teachers which benefits not only individual students but also the class as a whole. Whether a generic teacher provides special materials, demonstration, or in-class tutoring, assistance is provided to teachers in all academic areas as well as in behavior/classroom management.

As a coordinator, the generic teacher is, in effect, the single person within the school familiar with a student's total education program. The generic teacher works with principals, assistant principals, guidance counselors, teachers, parents, and students. Whereas a special education teacher or guidance counselor might perform case management-type duties, the generic teacher is in a more visible position, is more available, and can spend more time disseminating information and discussing specific students and their educational programs.

At the school level, personnel are introduced to the new generic teacher through staff development. Each session, led by the director of special education and the assigned mainstream teacher, lasts 60 to 90 minutes. The responsibilities of the generic teacher are presented, reserving a period of time for discussion.

In a preliminary evaluation of the effectiveness of the generic teacher model, results were favorable. Some teachers, especially the younger, less experienced teachers, reported that their frustrations were lessened by the generic teachers. Principals, teachers, and parents expressed satisfaction with the generic teacher's ability to be aware of the student's total educational program, performance, and behavior. In addition, guidance counselors at the secondary level feel that the generic teachers lessened their work load, thus providing them with more time to offer guidance services to students.

Generic teacher model II: The mainstream teacher. Another variation of the generic teacher is found in Belmont's neighbor, Cambridge, Massachusetts.

This LEA implements a form of the generic teacher model called the mainstream teacher.

Implementation of the mainstream teacher model follows several steps. Initially, the mainstream teachers acquaint themselves with their assigned schools by meeting staff in school lounges. Mainstream teachers emphasize the importance of this informal period to acquaint themselves with school procedures, policies, and politics and with "those in charge." A more formal introduction and explanation of the mainstream teacher's role is then provided during workshops presented in each school. Topics of discussion are: (a) the services to be provided by the mainstream teacher and (b) the concept of educating handicapped students in the regular classroom. Additional workshops include discussion regarding definitions and characteristics of mildly handicapped students and general information regarding modifications of academic programs.

Next, mainstream teachers initiate a needs assessment, surveying teachers' needs and desires for services provided by mainstream teachers. Some of the expressed needs result in workshops. Workshop topics have included individualized lesson planning techniques, behavior modification and classroom management strategies, diagnostic/prescriptive testing and teaching techniques, curriculum modification, and parent counseling. Some workshops were conducted by these mainstream teachers, others by outside consultants. Services provided by mainstream teachers were also listed and the list was provided to teachers and principals.

In their monitoring function, mainstream teachers convene and document at least two conferences per quarter with the classroom teachers of students who need special attention. It is suggested that at least two in-class observations of each student be made during that same period of time. Each mainstream teacher is required to complete a progress report for each student on a quarterly basis. Specific objectives are written for each student with the assistance of the classroom teacher for the teacher's own use. Thus, mainstream teachers provide direct services to teachers rather than to students, and educational planning takes place on an informal basis. Parents are involved in the educational planning process and their input is requested. However, the attendance of other special education personnel at informal planning meetings is optional.

Responses to the Cambridge mainstream teacher model are mixed. Elementary teachers report satisfaction with the mainstream teacher program, reporting that general teaching skills have been improved and that they feel less "threatened" by handicapped students. Secondary teachers are still rather skeptical about the appropriateness and usefulness of the program; they feel they are making too many concessions for mildly handicapped students.

Overall, however, the four mainstream teachers who are assigned to schools having 20 or more students with special needs are considered a welcome addition.

In summary, the use of the generic teacher model encourages the development of an effective interface between regular and special education. This model facilitates the provision of instructional services (direct and indirect) to special needs students and the provision of support services to regular educators.

Through use of the generic teacher model, Massachusetts' administrators offer a more effective service delivery system for teachers and students alike, thereby educating special needs students more appropriately in least restrictive environments.

Extra Mainstream Teachers As Floating Support Personnel

Another means of providing support to regular class teachers is through the employment of extra mainstream teachers in New Braunfels, Texas. In this strategy, extra mainstream teachers (EMTs), certified in special education, provide direct services to students on a flexible basis determined by each building principal. The functions they perform vary from school to school.

EMTs are assigned to elementary schools in New Braunfels which are heavily attended by handicapped students. While most principals prefer EMTs to work with students in regular classes as needed, one principal prefers to use the EMTs in a separate class (i.e., a resource room) with an assigned caseload. Generally, EMTs work as team teachers with regular class teachers who routinely integrate handicapped students into regular class activities. EMTs also work with students who are potential candidates for special education services.

Extra mainstream teachers provide tremendous support to the regular class teachers, thereby enabling greater numbers of handicapped children to be educated in less restrictive settings. This model also helps reduce the number of students referred to special education by providing indirect services to students served in the regular education environment. An added benefit is that it can promote positive teacher attitudes toward working with handicapped students in regular education settings.

Resource Specialists

One way the State of California has chosen to implement the LRE mandate is through the use of resource specialists as building-level special education generalists. This strategy, although used on a state-wide basis in California Master Plan districts, varies considerably from site to site. Services generally provided by the resource specialists include: (a) instruction to regular and/or special education students, (b) consultation with regular class teachers, (c) coordination of students' academic programs, and (d) inservice at the building level. In Contra Costa, California, the resource specialist is also viewed as the coordinator of special education activities on each campus.

Instructional service may be provided by the resource specialist in either of two curricular options and environments. Table 3 highlights the various possibilities. In cell A, the resource specialist may work with handicapped students either individually for approximately one hour daily or in small groups. The resource specialist who is working in the regular classroom may also instruct nonhandicapped students, using educational objectives which are being taught by the regular teacher. For cell B, the resource specialist is again working in the regular class, but is using separate materials to achieve different specific objectives, with similar long-term objectives as those of the regular teacher. Cell C shows the resource specialist working with the child in a special class using regular class curriculum, while students are taught with a different curriculum in a separate class in cell D. This framework varies considerably, depending on the orientation of district administrators, the building principal, the areas of expertise commended by each resource specialist, and the resource specialist's individual preferences on the delivery of instruction.

TABLE 3
Environmental and Curricular Options Implemented by the
California Resource Specialist

	Curricular Option	
Environment	*Reinforce Regular Class Curriculum*	*Work on Separate Curriculum*
Regular Education Class	A	B
Special Education Class	C	D

At least one resource specialist is assigned to each school so that specialists will be accessible to regular educators. This structure facilitates the discussion of emerging problems and possible solutions, the exchange of information and the distribution of materials. Thus, the resource specialist provides informal, in-service training at school buildings in addition to providing teachers with the support necessary to maintain mildly handicapped students in regular classes.

The resource specialist also coordinates children's educational programs during consultation and instructional periods. Information which assists in coordination activities is gained when the resource specialist conducts educational assessments. The resource specialist also "keeps a finger to the pulse of the school"—if problems or concerns arise at the building level, the resource specialist channels them to the principal, program specialist, or director of special education.

Resource specialists are viewed as the backbone of the building-level special education effort. The creation of this role has resulted in a reduction of the number of students served in special day classes and an increase in the overall number of students who received special education assistance.

Teacher Trainers

Worcester, Massachusetts, instituted a staff development team to address specific issues in the schools: mainstreaming, individualized instruction, and ethnicity and human relations. The three members of the team, referred to as teacher trainers, provide assistance to individual teachers and small groups in very specific curriculum areas. The positions are staffed with district personnel who are released from teaching responsibilities for the year. Contingent on school committee budget approval, the positions continue on a two-year rotating basis.

The original purpose of the teacher trainer position was to provide ongoing support to teachers to insure smooth integration of special needs students by modifying curriculum. This role has been modified, however, to more closely accommodate existing needs in the schools and to provide support to teachers of students who are potentially in need of special education services. Thus, while the emphasis remains on the regular classroom teacher and the modification of curriculum to accommodate individual needs, the service tends to focus on potential special needs situations. That is, the program has become more preventive in nature than was originally intended.

Teacher trainers are available to work with individual teachers and principals on request. Trainers report that they establish initial contact with principals and keep them informed of activities. The team meets on a weekly basis for planning and support. Team members reported that this interaction was most helpful in terms of sharing ideas and meeting the needs of the schools. Each teacher trainer maintains a weekly log of all contacts and the nature of the request, along with individual folders for each school which contains documentation of requests, plans, suggestions and follow-up.

Trainers attribute their success to several factors. First, since they were selected from district personnel, they were known to other staff. This promoted credibility; they are not viewed as "outside experts." Second, they are responsive and act promptly on requests. Third, the ongoing nature of the service promotes continued positive exchanges. Fourth, their positions are not part of special education, but of the staff development department.

Learning Center Teacher

Through the learning centers of Shawnee Mission, Kansas, a variety of services are made available to regular classroom teachers and to students with learning problems. The learning center teacher functions as an informal provider of support and information, a listening post, and a vehicle for communication for regular class teachers. On a more formal basis, the learning center teacher assists the regular class teacher in several ways: (a) planning, (b) developing modifications to the students' educational programs, (c) setting goals and designing written educational plans, (d) developing and using different teaching techniques, (e) incorporating a behavior modification program, or (f) teaching individual or small groups in the regular classroom. The learning center teacher maintains a communication link that is essential for program consistency.

In addition to the indirect services provided to the regular classroom teacher, the learning center teacher provides either direct instruction on a one-to-one or small group basis in the regular classroom or less than an hour per day one-to-one or small group instruction out of the regular classroom.

The learning center is not a mandated delivery system. Learning centers are established within individual school buildings when a building's administration and staff feel that the services afforded by such a center would be beneficial. When a building staff decides that a learning center is desired, a needs assessment is conducted to identify student, staff, and faculty service needs and supply and equipment needs.

Learning center services are provided to students on the basis of recommendation from the building screening committees; a full evaluation is not required. However, whenever more than one hour of specific skill instruction is provided to students identified as exceptional, a recommendation from the district screening committee, the approval of the student's parents, and a full evaluation must have been completed.

The learning center concept provides the opportunity for local building staff to work and plan together in order to more effectively provide for the needs of individual students. Since this is a cooperative strategy, it relies on communication and cooperation among the whole building staff and administration in order to serve students with an individualized, positive approach. In addition to the support provided by the learning center teacher, the learning center allows individual staff members with various areas of expertise to share their knowledge, materials, and resources with other staff members, thus facilitating the delivery of appropriate services to students in the least restrictive environment.

Supplemental Resource Instructors

The role of the supplemental resource instructor (SRI) in the Area Vocational Technical Institute (AVTI #916) in White Bear Lake, Minnesota, provides an interesting perspective on how support staff funded by special education can be effectively used to benefit all secondary students and teachers. The AVTI was created by state legislation in 1969 and has a full-service, individualized program that serves students from three counties. Students enrolled to the AVTI Center receive two to six weeks of assessment and vocational counseling. They are further prepared for a vocational program by role rehearsal, and then assigned to a regular vocational program for a tryout.

The role of the SRI was developed when further special education legislation was passed in Minnesota in 1971. The SRI's functions are to prepare students for the tryout, to monitor and provide direct instruction to both regular and special education students, and to consult with all teachers. As a monitor, the SRI uses a case management system to oversee the progress of all students while directing specific attention to the educational needs of the 30 students on his or her workload. It is the responsibility of the SRI to maintain communication between the home school and the AVTI and to coordinate the activities of students working in outside agencies.

As consultants, SRIs may provide materials and suggestions for vocational teachers to use with any student, not just those who have been identified as handicapped. In this function, they may be viewed as a resource and support to the teachers. SRIs also develop and modify curriculum (the curriculum of the AVTI is discussed in the next strategy).

As direct service providers, SRIs may team with other instructors to teach regular and handicapped students in the regular vocational program. Instruction may be provided at either the group or individual level; however, since the SRI's role is that of a support person, students are not removed to a separate class for this work. The SRI may also act as a counselor and advocate or conduct vocational assessments.

Part of the success of the SRI role in AVTI #916 has been the client-centered approach to education which is emphasized there. According to this approach, when problems occur "the instructor needs as much help as the child." It is the responsibility of the supplemental resource instructor to provide the appropriate resources needed to support each student's education. Under the basic philosophy that "slow learning is not in itself a handicap," that a noncompetitive structure is essential, and that a "normalized" environment is advantageous to all students, SRIs work to coordinate and support the education of all secondary students who attend this center.

Curriculum Developers

The AVTI also was the site of a second strategy, the coordination of curriculum development through instructional development specialists working in a Learning Resources Department. Emphasis is placed on the development of individual vocational learning packages for students. The Learning Resources Department is staffed with a coordinator, five instructional development specialists, and one staff development specialist. A district-wide priority list of program areas in which curriculum assistance is needed is developed each year on the basis of a needs assessment. Instructional development specialists are assigned to work on the high priority programs for 75% of their time. They are available to all teachers on a walk-in basis for the remaining 25% of their time. The coordinator noted that developers were essentially process-oriented and worked in close cooperation with the content-oriented instructors.

Skills needed by development specialists include an ability to work well with instructors, organizational skills, attention to detail, and strong writing skills. Instructional development specialists work with instructors to analyze the skills and activities needed by students to master the terminal curricular goal in each vocational content area. An instructor interview instrument is used to obtain the instructor's evaluation of his or her curriculum materials.

To ensure that individual classroom instructors engage in curriculum development activities, that function is included in all job descriptions. Three days per year are provided to instructors for curriculum development; a substitute teacher is hired to teach for those days. The Learning Resources Department is regarded as a service—developers are available to the instructors, and instructors are encouraged to use the developers' expertise. To reinforce this concept, the contract between the teachers bargaining unit and the district contains an incentive plan for curriculum development.

Overall, the AVTI's curriculum development process offers an innovative approach for assisting secondary teachers with the individualization of coursework for both regular and special education students. The coordination of regular and special curricula facilitates the integration of handicapped students and eases teachers' workloads. In addition to products developed for the AVTI, the Learning Resources Department has produced learning materials for use throughout the state, as well as nationally and internationally, and has produced materials under contract to private industry and government agencies.

Combining Administrative and Technical Assistance Functions

Other innovative personnel roles have been developed by combining some of the administrative functions described in this section with technical assistance functions to form a single personnel position. Roles with such combined functions may be particularly useful in small districts or where school buildings that require administrative or technical support are widely dispersed. Not all of these personnel positions are assigned to individual school buildings, however. Program specialists as used in California Responsible Local Agencies are one example.

Program Specialists

While not formally considered administrators, program specialists are hired through the responsible local agencies (RLAs) under the California Master Plan agreement to provide support to local school districts within the RLA. Program specialists were used in all Master Plan RLAs visited during this study; however, the role as it was implemented in Santa Barbara and Contra Costa form the basis for this description. It should be noted that the role of the program specialist, like that of the resource specialist, varied according to the needs of the RLA.

Coordinating and monitoring functions form the crux of the program specialist role. Program specialists serve as chairpersons for the educational assessment service team, coordinate the writing of the IEP, and assign case managers for all students who are assessed. In cases where children have severe handicapping conditions, the program specialist may serve as the case manager. The program specialist also conducts assessments of individual students, monitors individual students' instructional plans and, when necessary, recommends changes in these plans. When students are considered for placement in nonpublic school programs, or when a determination of program effectiveness is needed, the program specialist may assume these duties. To ensure fluid communication, program specialists meet with the special education director monthly.

As consultants, program specialists support resource specialists, principals, and counselors. Any one of these persons may call on a program specialist for assistance with materials or instructional techniques for use in individual cases. Program specialists also assist local school appraisal teams to review, refine, and supplement program plans; they may also help special day class teachers in curriculum design and development. On the district level, the program specialist may be contacted by districts to assist in the development of the total special education program.

The staff development component of the program specialist role is less accentuated. Program specialists participate in staff development sessions when requested to do so by the resource specialist or by an administrator. These staff development sessions are provided formally, in large groups or on a school-by-school basis, or informally, by department at the high school level.

Program specialists may have a specific area of expertise in one type of handicapping condition, or may be generalists with knowledge of all handicapping conditions. Each may be assigned to an entire multidistrict RLA (region) or to one district.

Facilitators

The St. Paul, Minnesota, School District developed the role of the facilitator to insure that recommended services for special needs students are delivered. The facilitators' role may be considered administrative, although they are viewed in the district as teachers on special assignment. Facilitators view their role as twofold: administrative (doing paperwork, holding conferences, etc.) and consultative (helping teachers, teaching regular educators who work with handicapped students, etc.).

When the facilitator position was first implemented, several steps were taken to assure its success. First, general guidelines on the new role were given to principals and facilitators. Then, jointly, these persons designed the role to meet the specific needs of the school. Second, six weeks of summer training was given to facilitators. They also received on-the-job training for two mornings a week in neighborhood schools. Summer salaries for facilitators were paid by the school district, and facilitators also developed a child study handbook. Third, facilitators were required to have a background in special education; they also found it helpful to receive additional training after a few months in their new roles. Fourth, a group of facilitators formed a self-support group. This group discussed problems, solutions, and general concerns.

In summary, the facilitators are viewed as a valuable resource. Some of the modifications to this role that have been suggested by facilitators are: (a) assign facilitators to only one building, (b) offer more specific training, and (c) offer training in administrative management. Facilitators felt that by being assigned to just one building they could offer more support to regular educators. This change would eliminate the duplication of many services in the building, since facilitators could be full-time building coordinators.

Special Education Consultants

Special education consultants provide diverse services to regular and special education administrative and instructional personnel as well as to parents. They relieve burdens from special education administrators in providing communication links and support services to school administrators and resource room teachers. They work with appraisal teams to insure a smooth transition from assessment to instructional placement. At the same time, they lessen the burdens of the resource room teacher in providing support and assistance to regular education teachers regarding the instruction of handicapped students in the regular education classroom. This assistance seems to result in more time spent in providing direct services to handicapped students and offers regular classroom teachers more assistance when working with handicapped students in their classrooms.

The intent of creating the role was to delegate responsibilities for communicating and providing professional support services to school administrators as well as to regular and special education staff. Special education consultants are assigned to elementary, middle, and senior high schools. They are not necessarily assigned to any one level of educational setting, but for example, may be assigned to two elementary schools and one high school. The consultants attempt to arrange their schedules so that they visit each school at least one day per week. Consultants also attempt to coordinate their activities so that the scheduled days at any given school remain constant. Since they take an active role in student assessment, placement, and dismissal meetings, the consultants consider consistent scheduling essential.

Although the description of the special education consultant's responsibilities was generally agreed on, it seemed that each consultant performed somewhat differently. Although only one consultant performed all the responsibilities listed below, this description indicates the great variety of services consultants offer.

- Make presentations to special education personnel at inservice training sessions.
- Help the regular education teachers acquire materials or modify existing materials and curricula.
- Discuss IEPs, materials, and classroom instructional methods with regular education teachers.
- Demonstrate materials and instructional methods for use with handicapped students in the regular classroom.
- Discuss student difficulties with regular and resource room teachers.
- Discuss individual students' problems with principals.
- Assist the resource room teacher in scheduling students and provide reminders for deadlines regarding required paperwork.
- Deliver materials and central office communications to resource room teachers.
- Substitute for the resource room teacher while he or she obtains materials from the LEA materials center.
- Discuss general manifestations of handicapping conditions and alternative teaching strategies with regular education teachers.

This mix of responsibilities reflects both the consultant's administrative functions—communicating with administrators and helping to coordinate regular and special education activities—and the consultant's technical support functions.

Special Education Liaison

The role redefinition of a regular education principal to that of special education liaison is one example of a strategy which was developed to meet communication and consultation needs. The liaison is responsible for communicating significant information to special and regular education administrators and staff and for providing technical assistance regarding the integration of handicapped students.

The nature of the consultant function for the special education liaison varies according to the needs of his or her target audience. When consulting with principals, the special education liaison may act as a participant in parent and student evaluation committee meetings at the principal's request. This may occur when: (a) the principal anticipates a difficult or controversial meeting due to previous disagreement between parents and the school, or (b) the nature of severity of the handicapping condition warrants extra consideration. The special education liaison may also consult with the building principal on legal issues and offer unofficial advice.

In consulting with regular and special education teachers, the special education liaison may, upon request, enter the classroom to observe the implementation of a student's education program and may offer suggestions regarding modification of materials and instructional techniques. Another alternative which the special education liaison may arrange is to have another teacher discuss and/or demonstrate materials and instructional techniques in the classroom. In addition, the special education liaison may discuss staff development needs with the teacher and assist in coordination of building-level presentations. This latter function was found to satisfy teacher needs for information on how to work with handicapped children while also providing the principal with some direction regarding his or her professional development responsibilities.

In planning for this position, several factors need to be considered. First, a known and respected regular education administrator should be considered for the position. This person should be experienced in programming for handicapped students, working with parents, and providing relevant assistance to teachers. It would be optimal for this person to be certified in both regular and special education.

Second, care should be taken to provide the special education liaison with a budget for materials. This could be arranged through a joint budget between the special and regular education departments as a line item for the position or provided as needed from the general supply fund. This person should also have access to a materials center.

Third, the special education liaison would need to compile a list of instructional specialists who would be available to assist him or her in consultation. These persons should have credibility with other faculty as well as the ability to provide an open atmosphere.

In summary, the role redefinition of a regular education administrator to that of special education liaison was found by this school district to further its ability to provide more appropriate education to handicapped students in less restrictive settings. The position resulted in consistency among school practices and procedures. School administrators also reported that with the role of special education liaison in operation they could better use their time.

Team Chairman

The role of the team chairman in Milford, Massachusetts, was created in 1974 by state mandate. The team chairman position merged the role of the generic teacher with that of the evaluation team chairperson. A team chairman facilitates the integration of mildly handicapped students into the least restrictive environment by acting as a coordinator within the school building and overseeing the referral to placement process. The chairman also offers support to the classroom teachers and eliminates unnecessary referrals.

The actual development of the chairman's role was flexible, but certain basic responsibilities were established. In an administrative capacity, the team chairman manages all paperwork involved in an evaluation team (ET) meeting, initiates the meeting, sends out the necessary forms, gathers permission forms, notifies participants of the meeting, conducts the meeting, and assists in development of the IEP.

The generic teacher portion of this role involves consulting with regular educators in making environmental and curricular modifications. Chairmen observe students, offer practical teaching and material suggestions and advise teachers on the referral process. The team chairman also conducts educational assessments for students referred as candidates for special education services.

To accomplish these many tasks, team chairmen found it necessary to schedule time in each building so that they were accessible to staff. A flexible schedule with accessibility to chairmen is of prime importance to teachers. Friday is usually reserved for staff meetings and the completion of paperwork. Planning meetings with the special education director are also held weekly.

In implementing the team chairman role, district administrators required team chairmen to be legally certified as generic teachers. Although no extensive training for this position was conducted by the district, some sessions were held on state law and the status of its implementation in the district.

Team chairmen are invaluable staff additions who function as direct extensions of the special education director. When chairmen are in school buildings they are able, in many cases, to offer immediate help to principals. With one person coordinating ET meetings, much confusion and paperwork have been eliminated for both principals and teachers.

Administrative and Technical Assistance Roles: Conclusion

The strategies presented in this section include new positions as well as redefined positions. In some cases, some of the functions fulfilled by these personnel roles were similar. It is interesting to note that in designing these positions, administrators in different states felt the need to fill similar functions, yet they have often assigned these functions to different personnel roles in accordance with the unique aspects of their service delivery structures. Table 4 shows the functions assigned to each of these personnel and the levels at which they work (building, area, district, or multidistrict region).

The table shows that personnel roles assigned to the district or multidistrict regional level are generally assigned a smaller number of functions to perform over a broader area. Surprisingly, however, the particular functions do not appear to be allied with levels of assignment. For example, both the facilitators and the resource specialists coordinate the delivery of special education services and provide information and materials to individual teachers. However, several facilitators perform these functions for the entire district of St. Paul, while one resource specialist works at each building in Contra Costa, California. District characteristics and service delivery structures undoubtedly affect these assignments, but it is also of interest that the role of facilitator includes a third function (maintaining federal reporting data) that requires district-wide coordination.

In creating or redefining these personnel roles, administrators have had to consider the needs of their districts in terms of the functions to be filled and the appropriate grouping of those functions into positions that would work within their unique service delivery structures. Related considerations include whether positions should be itinerant or building based, whether they are best filled by full- or part-time personnel, and how many positions are needed in order to adequately perform those functions within the district.

Many of the position descriptions of this section reflect special concern for providing communication among personnel who hold building based or itinerant positions. In many strategies, regularly scheduled meetings with the director of special education were the vehicle for coordination among personnel in the same position as well as for coordination with special education administration.

Certain roles, such as California's resource and program specialists, require knowledge of the district. That is, in order to adequately perform their functions, these personnel had to be familiar with district programs and practices and had to have established credibility with their colleagues. Thus, both of these positions were filled with current district personnel.

In addition, both of these positions required special training. Thus, further considerations in both creating and redefining positions are the skills and knowledge required to fill the functions needed by the district. On that basis, special training or ongoing consultation (as is required by rotating positions such as that of teacher trainers) can be provided. Specific techniques for providing staff development are discussed in the next chapter.

TABLE 4
Functions and Levels of Personnel Roles

Personnel Role	Maintains federal reporting data	Keeps track of current events	Meets regularly with district administrators	Coordinates special and regular education	Coordinates delivery of special ed. services	Coordinates students' programs	Coordinates evaluation process	Places students with postschool needs	Performs building-level needs assessment	Works with building administrators	Communicates with parents	Participates in IEP meetings	Monitors special education in-service	Provides, contributes to sp. ed. in-service	Provides information, materials to teachers	Establishes and maintains resource room	Demonstrates instructional techniques in class	Observes classes	Develops curricula, assists in modification	Instructs students	Building	Area	District	Multidistrict Region
Special Education Area Representative	X	X	X	X	X							X	X									X		
Evaluation Team Chairperson							X	X			X	X									X			
Dually Certified Teacher				X							X									X	X			
Generic Teacher Model I															X		X			X	X			
Generic Teacher Model II: Mainstream Teacher									X	X		X		X	X	X					X			
Extra Mainstream Teacher		X				X								X	X			X			X			
Resource Specialist					X							X		X	X				X	X	X			
Teacher Trainer														X	X				X		X			
Learning Center Teacher																			X		X		X	
Supplemental Resource Instructor						X													X	X				X
Instructional Development Specialist						X	X												X					X
Program Specialist					X	X	X					X		X	X				X					X
Facilitator	X						X												X	X				X
Special Education Consultant			X				X					X		X	X		X	X	X	X			X	
Special Education Liaison			X	X								X		X	X		X	X	X				X	
Team Chairman							X								X			X	X				X	

"Functions may vary; those shown here are typical.

It is important to note, however, that all of these decisions stem from consideration of the needs of the school district and its organizational and service delivery structures. Provision of clear role guidelines and the administrative support, training, and consultation needed were requirements for each position. Although the functions encompassed by the positions described here are often similar, each position has been tailored to the specific situation that exists in a district.

STRATEGIES FOR USING TEAM TEACHING AND PARAPROFESSIONALS

Team Teaching Strategies

The assignment of special educators to teaching teams can be an excellent mechanism to facilitate the integration of mildly handicapped students. In addition to having the capability to provide handicapped students with special instructional assistance as needed, such teams are also better able to provide handicapped students with additional help in particular problem areas on an informal basis. Since the inclusion of a special educator on the team expands the team's range of expertise, such teaming can also benefit both regular and special teachers by offering an excellent opportunity to share their respective fields of knowledge. The strategies described in this section illustrate several types of teaching teams that were developed to address specific needs.

Teaming of Secondary Regular and Special Educators

Galveston, Texas, implemented a teaming strategy to facilitate the integration of handicapped high school students into English and math classes. Regular classroom teachers who volunteer to participate in the program work cooperatively with special education teachers assigned to regular classes for four periods daily.

Responsibilities of the special educator include direct instructional assistance to handicapped students and demonstration of alternative teaching styles. In the team teaching situation, a 25:2 student-to-teacher ratio is maintained; the class ratio for single instructors was 20:1. Handicapped students are assigned on a random basis to classes instructed by the teams.

Although this strategy did facilitate mainstreaming, there were some problems with its implementation. Regular and special educators lacked training in team teaching. Also, no specific portion of the day had been reserved for cooperative planning time. For these reasons, it was not uncommom to find one teacher assuming many of the responsibilities for the classroom. Furthermore, no guidelines were offered to the teachers involved. While special educators were assigned to classrooms, regular educators in the program were volunteers. (Administrators considered this to be a nonthreatening approach to regular educators.) Another drawback was that little time was provided for staff development. Teachers suggested that this effort could be improved if all teachers were offered support in the form of knowledge of team teaching with attention to methods, secondary curriculum, and planning skills.

In addition to administrative support, personalities and professionalism are an integral factor in the success of this strategy, contributing largely to its several benefits. The strategy helps to increase students' self-concepts, and special education teachers no longer feel isolated. Rather, they function as active members of the staff. Regular education students are no longer reluctant to confer with special education teachers, since special educators are not labeled as teachers of the handicapped.

Teaming Among Dually Certified Personnel

This strategy from St. Paul, Minnesota, teams special education teachers who are dually certified in special education and a regular high school subject area. This enables the special education staff to work cooperatively with teachers in the other curriculum areas to facilitate the integration of handicapped students.

This strategy was begun three years ago in an attempt to build a cooperative effort between two departments. The first team established was a voluntary one since, initially, few teachers had an interest in working with special education teachers. Now many teachers, both regular and special, request such teaming. Together, they actively plan the curriculum, making suggestions for modifications for all students.

With this strategy, two full-time and one part-time special education teachers and one mainstream management aide work with approximately 65 handicapped students who are integrated into regular classes. Teaching is conducted by both the regular educator and the special educator within the regular class environment.

The response to this strategy is very favorable. Teachers are extremely pleased. Students are sharing and helping one another. And underlying these responses is the fact that the distance between special and regular education has been bridged.

Placement of a Special Educator on the Teaching Team

In 1972, St. Paul, Minnesota, instituted a comprehensive program to individualize instruction for all children. Over a four-year period, all buildings in the district were phased into the program. Team teaching was one of the key components of the model. The placement of special education teachers on regular education teaching teams was inherent in the philosophy of a program of education to meet the needs of each child. Identified children were assigned to a team and all members shared responsibility for all students.

To implement this strategy, the superintendent and assistant superintendent, with support from the regional education center, developed long-range plans for the district-wide program. One school was chosen to pilot the program. It was announced that all positions in that pilot school were open and all teachers in the district were invited to apply. The staff was thus selected carefully and their commitment to the program was high. Modifications of the school environment were made in order to provide a facility with plenty of open space. Teachers were assigned to teams of three to five members which included special teachers. The faculty was involved in extensive staff development in the school's instructional program.

Over a four-year period, all buildings in the district experienced similar instructional and environmental changes. The decision to have the special educators on the teaching teams has been effective in integrating handicapped youngsters. The team works as a group with the goal of serving every child. Special education personnel have primary responsibility for the special education students as well as for regular education youngsters. Conversely, regular education teachers work with special education children. The special needs teacher also provides support and informal inservice to team members. One principal noted that in practice, "all team members shared their expertise and both regular and special educators grew professionally."

Preclass Approach to Team Teaching

Another team teaching strategy with two distinct variations was implemented in Red Wing, Minnesota. The first variation was implemented when declining enrollment at the junior high level resulted in a reduced case load for one industrial education instructor and one home economics teacher, thus freeing both teachers for one period daily. During this extra time, the special education resource room teacher worked with the two regular education teachers to provide a preclass session for special education students. Before students were assigned to regular classes, they attended preclass sessions to develop preparatory skills that would help to ensure their success in the regular class program.

The payoff of this program is that it provides support to the regular teacher working with special education students. The process ensures that the experiences of regular class teachers working with handicapped students were initially controlled and positive. Thus, teachers are better able to address the needs of students who are part of the regularly scheduled class. For handicapped youth, the preclass sessions provide an opportunity to become familiar with expectations and procedures of the regular class before they enter that environment.

It should be noted that the cooperation between regular and special education was first made possible in large measure through the decline in student enrollment. Were enrollment figures to drastically increase, the time needed within the school day to implement this strategy might disappear. If enrollment were to decrease sharply, the personnel positions might be altogether eliminated. Therefore, the provision of services under these two arrangements is highly dependent on scheduling concerns and on the faculty to student ratio.

The major outcomes from this effort are twofold. For students enrolled in the junior high resource program, the preclass sessions permit them to experience success in a supportive environment, which facilitates their success in the regular academic program. For teachers, the preclass sessions provide experience in team teaching as well as experience in providing appropriate services to handicapped students in least restrictive settings. Red Wing administrators indicate that this strategy also serves to communicate the willingness of special education staff to support regular education teachers in meeting the needs of all students with special needs who are served within their classrooms.

Summary: Teaming Strategies

These strategies represent the efforts of a variety of school districts to promote the integration of mildly handicapped students by providing more appropriate and coordinated instruction to all students. The Galveston teaming approach, teaming among dually certified personnel, placement of a special educator on the teaching team, and the preclass approach to team teaching may be implemented at the secondary level. Using a special educator as a member of a teaching team and the learning center may also be implemented at the elementary level.

An important point to keep in mind when using teaming approaches is the provision of necessary administrative support in terms of training, guidelines, and planning time. The reassignment of personnel and introduction of a new instructional delivery model is not in itself sufficient to ensure acceptance and success. When introducing changes, personnel must be given adequate support and skill to adapt to those changes. If administrative support in these forms is not adequate, teachers will not feel successful and the potential benefits of this model may not be realized.

Paraprofessionals

Paraprofessionals can support the integration of handicapped students in regular classes and can allow teachers greater flexibility in instructional arrangements. For example, by working with students on an individual or small group basis, paraprofessionals can provide students with more individual attention when that type of assistance is required. The strategies presented in this section illustrate the benefits which may be accrued through the employment of paraprofessionals, teaching assistants, or teaching aides.

Teacher Aides to Manage Paperwork

Integrating handicapped students into regular education environments may increase the paperwork demanded of regular education teachers. To alleviate this situation and free the teaching staff to perform their instructional functions effectively, West Columbia, Texas, assigned aides to teachers who integrated handicapped students in their classes. After their introduction to district procedures and initial training, aides rely on the teacher to whom they are assigned for additional direction. In all instances, aides complete the necessary paperwork for the ongoing program of the student. Since this amounts to 20–25% of the estimated paperwork which teachers were responsible for completing, teachers view the use of aides as most helpful. In some cases, aides are able to assume almost all paperwork responsibilities, thus freeing the teacher to spend more time in direct instruction.

Districts implementing this strategy would, of course, need funds to pay for teacher aides and their initial training. However, with the increased amount of paperwork necessitated by the integration and monitoring of handicapped students in regular classrooms, this strategy is an effective mechanism for providing support to regular class teachers.

Instructional Aides

In Massachusetts, an overabundance of certified teachers has led to the employment of instructional aides qualified to instruct students who require the one-to-one or small group work in the resource room. This has enabled special educators to move into regular classrooms in order to meet the needs of additional handicapped students. The special education teacher develops the educational plan, establishes weekly objectives, provides appropriate materials, and monitors students' progress. The instructional aide implements the preestablished program in the resource room. A list of students to be served by the instructional aide is approved by the director of special education to insure that the needs of these students can be met through this arrangement.

According to the educators interviewed in Lynnfield, Massachusetts, most of the students served by the instructional aides require one-to-one and/or small group work because of short attention spans and distractibility, not because of severe handicapping conditions. For these students, a different educational environment and educational plan can be a quite effective intervention. The special education teacher monitors each student's progress weekly on a formal basis, but informal interaction between the special educator and instructional aide occurs almost daily.

A secondary benefit of the instructional aide model is that it frees the special education teacher to work in regular classes with students whose needs may be less severe, yet who still require the assistance of the special educator. Previously, these students were either inappropriately served in the resource room (a too-restrictive environment) or not served at all (because of limited resources).

In summary, expanded services and more intensive, appropriate services were not the only benefits to be achieved from using instructional aides in the resource room. Instructional aides free the special education teacher to work in regular classes, so that communication between regular and special educators is enhanced. Opportunities for regular and special educators to work together and to discuss problems and progress were increased. In addition, the regular class teacher has an opportunity to observe the methods and techniques used by the special educator. As regular educators develop increased awareness of the role of the special educator, many of their concerns regarding what occurs during the student's sessions with the special educator may be eliminated.

Another major benefit to emerge from the use of the instructional aide was the more appropriate programming that became available to students who require the services of the special educator, but who do not require the environment of the resource room.

Mainstream Management Aides Assigned to Students

The role of the mainstream management aide was created in St. Paul, Minnesota, to provide extra support for both handicapped students and their regular class teachers. Mainstream management aides are assigned to elementary schools on the basis of the number of IEPs that indicate they are needed. Although a majority of the aides function at the elementary level, some provide assistance to secondary students. Aides work with students in regular classrooms, offering support to individual students and small or large groups while the classroom teacher works with the remaining students.

The role of the mainstream aide is primarily instructional, although it may also involve modifying materials for the regular class teacher and functioning as a communications link between the regular and special education programs. Support to students takes the form of guiding independent work activities and assuring the safety of students as they move from one environment to another (e.g., learning center to physical education class). The instructional activities of the mainstream management aide consist primarily of working with handicapped students individually or in small groups on academic assignments. The aide might also demonstrate instructional methods for use with handicapped students.

Several qualifications for the position of mainstream management aide are required in St. Paul. They are as follows: (a) experience as a classroom aide, (b) experience with handicapped students, (c) training relevant to mainstreaming through formal course work (or willingness to participate in such training while employed), (d) willingness and ability to follow educational prescriptions as presented in the IEP or orally by a supervising teacher, and (e) willingness to participate in an evaluation of the mainstream management aide's pilot program. The main drawback of the mainstream management aide strategy as implemented in St. Paul seems to occur in salary negotiations. These persons are paid the minimum wage and it is difficult to recruit people for the position at that salary level.

The role of the mainstream management aide as operationalized in the St. Paul schools illustrates the effect that well-selected support staff can have on maintaining handicapped students in regular education environments. Both regular and special education teachers are pleased with the benefits of the new role. It is felt that with the mainstream management aide, the quality of service the handicapped student receives is greatly enhanced.

Technical Tutors

Like the supplemental resource instructor role discussed earlier, the technical tutor is a vocational education role. The role was created to remedy the difficulty in placing handicapped students into regular vocational programs and to support handicapped students after their placement in the vocational setting. Like the supplemental resource instructor (SRI) role previously presented, the role of the technical tutor is one of instruction and support. However, the SRI role is one which stresses these activities in a large center which draws students from three counties; the technical tutor model operates in only one school district. The technical tutor works in coordination with the facilitator to provide vocational assessment. The majority of students with whom technical tutors work are classified as learning disabled.

When necessary, the tutor develops and modifies curriculum or equipment to support the student in the mainstream environment. Tutors obtain academic, medical, and behavioral information from the student's IEP, and also conduct their own assessments through direct experience with the student. Often, a student's educational program is further supported by communication with the student's home school; this, too, is a responsibility of the technical tutor.

One of the major problems of this strategy is that tutors are paid as paraprofessionals. This makes it difficult to recruit highly qualified people to work for the salary; it also fosters some feelings of resentment on the tutors' behalf.

A workshop was held to help begin the technical tutor program. Now an educational assistant is hired for 26 hours weekly to advise and offer suggestions to technical tutors. Although implementation varies with each vocational program, tutors usually work with facilitators and individual students. At times, tutors also assist vocational teachers.

In-School Suspension Program Paraprofessionals

An in-school suspension program implemented in Lynnfield, Massachusetts, represents an interesting use of paraprofessionals. Two half-day paraprofessionals are hired to supervise the program. They are scheduled so that their shifts overlap in order to ensure communication and consistency. These paraprofessionals may supervise up to five students at one time, although normally only one to three students are in attendance. Students are not forced to attend the in-school suspension program, but when their behavior warrants such a decision, the assistant principal may request that they attend. Students who do not wish to participate in the program are suspended from school and suffer the normal consequences.

The program provides academic tutoring in order to prevent the suspension from creating further academic failure and reducing the student's chances for success in school. In fact, the one-to-one tutoring that is available is thought to be responsible for actually improving the academic performance of some students. Since the paraprofessionals maintain communication with the students' teachers, continuity and remediation tailored to meet the students' needs are provided in an environment free from normal classroom distractions. The provision of individual assistance in an environment that has few distractions can help students to attain skills and understand concepts that might be difficult for them to attain in a different setting.

It should be noted that this personnel role was documented in Massachusetts, where there is an overabundance of certified teachers. Although the role was designed for paraprofessionals, it was filled in Lynnfield with certified teachers, and this situation contributed to the high quality of programming.

Summary

The roles presented in this section illustrate a variety of ways to use paraprofessionals. In addition to acting as teachers' administrative or instructional assistants, paraprofessionals can also be used in independent settings with the support and assistance of their students' classroom teachers. When paraprofessionals are assigned to independent settings, strong communication and coordination with the classroom teacher is essential.

When there is a shortage of certified teaching personnel, paraprofessionals can support and supplement teachers, lightening their burden. The strategies of this section have shown, however, that paraprofessionals are also useful in situations where there is an excess of certified teaching personnel. Although an overabundance of certified teachers is unfortunate for the teachers themselves, their employment as paraprofessionals provides them with an opportunity to work with students, to add to their experience, and to be of benefit to both the students and the district. The use of such highly qualified personnel can increase both the quality of the program to which they are assigned and the amount of support provided to their coworkers.

Team Teaching and Paraprofessional Strategies: Conclusion

In this chapter, a variety of strategies which emphasize the roles of professionals involved with the education of all children, particularly handicapped children, has been presented. These strategies have addressed two areas. Team teaching strategies and a variety of uses of paraprofessionals as members of the instructional team were presented. The utilization of these strategies is addressed here.

Strategies for Teaming

The teaming strategies presented in this section represent approaches toward enhancement of the instructional process through shared instructional activities, planning, and expertise. St. Paul implemented two teaming strategies. One of these emphasized the use of dually certified teachers at the secondary level, while the other highlighted the coordination of each child's instructional program by a team of professionals. One model found in Red Wing, Minnesota, operated at the junior high level by allowing special education instructors to work with regular teachers for one period daily to establish a preclass for handicapped students. In Galveston, Texas, teachers of regular subject matter areas teamed with special educators to instruct both special and regular students assigned to the regular classroom.

In contrast to the positions described in the first part of the chapter, teaming strategies are useful within all types of district administrative structures. The organization of the LEA and its relationship to the SEA or intermediate unit appears unimportant. However, all strategies except the use of the special educator on the teaching team are best suited for districts which have an abundance of training personnel currently available. All teaming strategies may be quickly implemented.

Strategies for Using Paraprofessionals

Five strategies specifically directed toward the efficient use of paraprofessionals in the educational process were presented. The use of instructional aides and the use of paraprofessionals in the in-school alternatives to suspension program presented ideas for using paraprofessionals to supplement and complement the roles of the regular instructional staff. The mainstream management aides and the technical tutors in St. Paul acted as support personnel. The former worked with students whose IEPs called for this special help and the latter provided instruction to students in vocational programs and support to the vocational educator in planning the instructional program. The use of teacher aides in West Columbia was designed to alleviate a portion of the paperwork which was overwhelming to many instructors.

All of the paraprofessional and aide roles presented within this chapter are implemented as easily where a personnel shortage exists as they are where qualified personnel are abundant. They can also be easily used in small, urban, or widely dispersed areas. Building space availability is not usually a concern in implementing these roles, since most paraprofessionals work within existing classrooms. An exception to this is the in-school suspension paraprofessionals strategy, which needs classroom space for the program.

Strategy characteristics which are important to consider in implementing paraprofessional roles include the level of within-district coordination, personnel, support, funding, and the time which must be allotted for planning and implementation. On the dimension of coordination, the in-school suspension program paraprofessionals and the mainstream management aides require coordination at the district and building levels as well as within classrooms. However, use of the technical tutor requires coordination at the first two levels but not at the classroom level. The instructional aide strategy requires within-building and classroom coordination, while use of teacher aides to manage paperwork requires only within-classroom coordination.

All uses of paraprofessionals to facilitate the integration of handicapped students require the addition of new personnel with different skills to the local education agency system. In addition, all of these strategies require ongoing consultation with the exception of the suspension program paraprofessionals.

This same strategy and the technical tutor require substantial funds, while the remaining three roles require minimal funding. Each paraprofessional strategy may be quickly implemented.

CONCLUSION

This chapter has presented a variety of strategies which are diverse in nature and implementation, while singular in their final intent: facilitating the education of all students in the most appropriate, least restrictive environment. While the impetus for changes in roles and responsibilities may be attributed in large measure to the influx of innovations in the area of special education, they cannot be assumed to have been developed solely to meet the needs of special education students.

Over the past decade, the growth of special education has provided the opportunity for both regular and special education administrators to review their long-range plans for the education of students and to make bold changes in the delivery systems which they offer to meet the needs of the individual handicapped and nonhandicapped student. Legislation such as Public Law 94-142 and Section 504 has provided a psychological as well as a legal incentive for administrators to proceed with innovations which they may once have felt were too radical to be accepted. Having now created their opportunities, administrators are responding to the mandate for education in most appropriate, least restrictive environments in a number of innovative and district-specific ways.

One dramatic indication of this administrative response is the number of new roles and functions which both regular and special educators are assuming to meet the needs of individual students in a coordinated fashion. The strategies presented in this chapter should be seen as prototypic in nature; they should be used to encourage the development of additional creative responses to the diversity of needs of local education agencies throughout the nation.

REFERENCE

Harris, B.M., & Bessent, W. *In-service education: A guide to better practice.* Englewood Cliffs NJ: Prentice-Hall, 1969.

5

Staff Development

SUSAN E. ELTING

Public Law 94-142 has become an influential precursor of in-service training programs in both state and local education agencies. The law draws a direct relationship between the least restrictive environment provision and training; it also places governance of these activities with the state educational agency. It states:

> Each state educational agency shall carry out activities to insure that teachers and administrators in all public agencies are fully informed about their responsibilities for implementing §300a.550, and are provided with technical assistance and training necessary to assist them in this effort. (§300.a555)

In addition, the comprehensive system of personnel development provision (§300a.380) has broad implications for in-service training which can be expected to affect LRE practices directly and indirectly. State mandates and regulations expand and reinforce the importance of in-service education (ISE) as an instrument for bringing about change in education. As Clifford (1978) emphasizes, mainstreaming as *public policy* for education demands change.

Many writers agree with Timpane's (1978) observation that "we are creating a new educational system; the present opportunity is unique, it will not recur." Joyce and his colleagues (Joyce, Howey, Yarger, Hill, Waterman, Vance, Parker, & Baker, 1976) note three areas of change which are currently affecting the schools: multicultural education, mainstreaming, and the early childhood education movement. They state, "Mainstreaming really involves a change in the atmosphere of the school, its organization and the type of community that is developed within it."

While LEAs seem consistent in providing activities under the broad rubric of in-service education, there is considerable variation in the process and content of these activities. Viewed collectively, the strategies for in-service training are widely discrepant with regard to such issues as purpose, terminology, definition, method of delivery, and service sphere.

Previous chapters of this handbook have emphasized the need for comprehensive planning and strong communications to support the merger of the special education and regular education domains. The integration of special education in-service training activities into a comprehensive, planned, and coordinated system with regular education in-service activities is a vital part of this support. The first section of this chapter presents strategies for planning in-service training activities that emphasize the integration of special education in-service within a comprehensive system and obtain input from a broad range of personnel.

Staff development which takes place in the context of the actual classroom is also an important form of support to the integration of handicapped students. Strategies which utilize job-embedded staff development are discussed in the second section of this chapter.

The third and final section presents innovative examples of a more traditional form of in-service education: job-related staff development. In addition to workshops and seminars, this category includes teacher centers, exchanges, and visitations. Thus, the strategies discussed in this chapter represent a diversity of purposes and delivery methods.

PLANNING STAFF DEVELOPMENT PROGRAMS

Planning for staff development programs requires the elements for success noted in Chapter 1: a range of knowledgeable personnel and adequate time. As in Chapter 1, the focus of this section is integrated planning to support the merger of the special and regular education domains. Thus, comprehensiveness is the focus of these strategies, and comprehensiveness is viewed from a variety of perspectives.

First, a flexible state policy for staff development and its diverse implementation in four districts is described. This part illustrates the importance of a comprehensive, state-wide philosophy toward the integration of handicapped students, and also portrays the need for flexibility in such a policy so that it may be adapted to the unique needs, structures, and styles of individual districts.

Next, strategies that use committee approaches to planning are presented. Committee structures can provide an opportunity to represent a broad range of staff and can thereby integrate the concerns of personnel working in diverse components of the educational system.

The importance of a wide range of staff input to in-service training plans cannot be overstated. In order to develop activities that address a realistic array of needs, staff must be consulted to determine the nature of those needs. Additionally, the methods and procedures used to convey information can best be told by the recipients of the information. The third and final part of this section provides additional strategies for obtaining staff input.

Varied Implementations of State Policy

According to Public Law 94-142, state education agencies have a central role in the governance of professional development activities. Minnesota offers an interesting illustration of how a state may take the initiative in setting the policy for such a program and how regional and local agencies operationalize that policy.

The 1976 Minnesota State Legislature enacted a law (M.S. 123.581) and appropriated funding for pilot programs for the in-service training of regular classroom teachers in techniques of educating mildly learning disabled and mildly retarded pupils. The following year, that legislation was amended to include in-service training programs for regular classroom teachers, assistant principals and principals. These appropriations underscored the state's commitment to the provision of services to handicapped students in the least restrictive environment. Program proposals could be submitted by cooperating districts in special education regional councils, educational cooperative service units or single districts. The four models presented here represent each of these options and illustrate how the Minnesota mandate was operationalized.

Cooperative Planning for District Staff Development Programs

The model implemented in Mankato is an example of cooperating districts in a special education regional council initially working together to explore some alternatives and then pursuing those alternatives at the district level. During the 1976–1977 school year, a regional mainstreaming in-service committee was formed to study a variety of plans for educating mildly handicapped children in the least restrictive educational environment. The special education director and the elementary and secondary staff development coordinators from the Mankato School District served as members of this regional committee. An initial activity of the committee was to review existing training materials which might serve regional goals. They decided to use existing programs rather than to develop new training packages. Consultants familiar with programs were contacted and invited to meet with the committee to further explain the programs under consideration.

Concurrent with the regional committee meetings, the Mankato staff development coordinators met with district personnel to discuss training needs and potential programs to meet those needs. At least five group meetings were held at the building level during this period. At the final committee meeting, it was decided to adopt the Learning Opportunities for Teachers (LOFT) training program to meet the mainstreaming needs at the local district level in the region.

Once the decision on a training program was reached, the regional special education coordinator initiated plans to begin the training of trainers during a one-week workshop as part of the pilot regional program. Each of the administrative units in the region selected participants to attend the training session.

Mankato selected a corps of four trainers to attend the workshop. They included the elementary and secondary staff development coordinators, one high school teacher, and one severe behavior and learning problems (SBLP) consultant.

On the basis of this experience and feedback on training needs within the district, the special education director in Mankato developed a proposal for local implementation during the 1977–1978 school year. The proposal was submitted to the State Board of Education and was approved for funding.

Trainers began to develop and prepare in-service materials for the workshops. They were released from teaching responsibilities for at least 10 school days in order to expand the kit into a functional set of working materials for the workshops. An evaluation instrument was developed to provide participant feedback.

The district training team and the training consultant met with all district administrators to give them basic exposure to the program. Following this briefing session, a letter explaining the substance of the program was sent to all faculty and administrators in the district. The letter inviting volunteer participation was sent jointly from the elementary director, secondary director, and special education director and provided details on the program's expectations for participants, professional credit available (15 renewal credits for recertification), and the schedule of inservice training sessions. Interested teachers were asked to notify their principals if they wanted to participate. Principals each selected three staff members to participate in the first workshop. Once the teachers were selected, the district-level activity was initiated. The 19 participants were released from instructional responsibilities for the first workshop, which lasted one week. The training consultant was available for the initial two days of the session to provide feedback and support to the training team as the workshop progressed. Two additional training sessions were held that year.

For the Mankato district, information on staff needs and alternatives for filling those needs came from several sources, including the special education regional council and its consultants and discussions with district personnel. After the initial pilot workshop, an additional and essential form of information—feedback—was obtained from attendees. The final proposal to the state was developed on the basis of information from all of these sources and experience from these developmental stages. This information and experience contributed enormously to the success of the training program. This strategy also represents an additional organizational structure for the planning of staff development activities, since it combines the work of the regional council with the work of the individual district.

Mainstream Connection

The Little Falls District also became involved in a multidistrict, regional development effort. Regional cooperatives are particularly appropriate for rural, sparsely populated areas and the regional nature of the activity was sustained throughout this in-service training effort. The in-service education plan described here is part of a two-region effort which involved 438 elementary and secondary teachers, from 48 school districts within eight special education cooperatives.

The in-service project was designed to provide general knowledge and understanding, then to provide specific information on instructional methodology, and finally, to provide opportunities for application and practice. Project start-up activities began in September, and the first two months were used to employ staff, to establish communication with eight cooperatives, to secure required decisions from the governing boards of each cooperative, to develop appropriate instructional content, and to package that content.

Faculty for the training sessions were selected from project staff, university special education faculty, regular education classroom teachers and consultants, special education personnel with expertise in mainstreaming activities, and other special education consultants.

This example of cooperative planning is especially appropriate for rural areas, since both planners and trainees can be brought from a larger geographical area to participate in in-service activities. Activities can thus be better coordinated throughout the region and planning and development costs may be distributed across numerous small districts, enabling them to offer more comprehensive or elaborate training than each could afford separately.

This project was organized into three phases: an introduction to exceptionalities, methodology and strategies for curriculum modification, and a practicum experience. During Phase 1, participants attended four instructional meetings at which the needs and characteristics of handicapped children in the regular classroom and methods of programming for them were discussed. The sessions included lectures, demonstrations, simulations, and audiovisual presentations delivered by university faculty, local staff, and consultants.

Phase 2 activities consisted of four workshop-type sessions. Content of the sessions varied for elementary and secondary level participants. At the elementary level, the workshop focused on developing techniques for modifying reading, mathematics, and other subject matter areas and techniques in classroom management. At the secondary sessions, participants were organized into interest groups in which they learned specific instructional techniques to meet the needs of handicapped children in secondary programs.

Phase 3 activities asked participants to apply at least one instructional practice learned during Phase 2. In addition, participants were asked to maintain a log regarding their experiences and to report their experiences to other project participants.

The program evaluation indicated that participants showed an increase in knowledge regarding the needs and characteristics of handicapped children and learned new skills regarding instructional and curricular modification. Although the principal attitude instrument used by the project evaluator indicated no significant attitudinal change, a number of participants did indicate on self-rating instruments that they felt their attitudes were more positive as a result of the training received.

Cooperative planning of in-service activities can serve various purposes for a group of school districts. Single districts also responded to the Minnesota mandate. The activities of two such districts are discussed below.

Mainstream In-Service Project

St. Paul, as a large, urban area, chose to develop a district-wide program but placed emphasis on building-level development. This project was intended to provide in-service training and technical assistance to the principal and staff of each building so that they could develop and implement a "comprehensive mainstreaming plan." The training program was designed in cooperation with the local university under a grant from the state education agency.

The training was designed primarily for regular education personnel. In order to convey the commitment of the district to this project, the assistant superintendents of elementary and secondary education served as project directors. The planning process was initiated when the project advisory board was required by the state legislation to select a training specialist to coordinate the project.

The training was designed cooperatively by the school district and the University of Minnesota and was based on an introductory course, Mainstreaming: Issues for Individualizing Instruction, for regular education teachers. The training specialist had the responsibility for assisting principals to determine needs in the schools and planning programs. The University of Minnesota had responsibility for training a cadre of St. Paul school staff as adjunct faculty members to give the introductory course. During the first year of the project, five faculty members were trained to teach the introductory course and supervised by university staff throughout the year. The project was piloted in seven schools in the district.

During the second year, eight more adjunct faculty members, including regular classroom teachers and a principal, were trained and assigned to apprenticeship roles with experienced adjunct faculty. Thirteen additional training sites were selected. Also during the second year, principals and other administrators received courses in the management of mainstreaming. In-service training and consultation were made available to special education teachers and support staff to increase their awareness of the information and skills needed to facilitate mainstreaming and provide support to regular educators.

Having thus provided for in-service training to key staff, emphasis was shifted to follow-through activities leading to a coordinated mainstreaming plan for each school. Adjunct faculty members worked directly with principals to facilitate change in the schools. A second project training specialist was hired to work with the secondary schools. The two specialists provided technical assistance to principals and staff and coordinated mainstreaming efforts in the district.

In two years, the school district trained a cadre of staff members who were "well-versed in mainstreaming" to assist principals and teachers. Teachers from half the elementary schools and one quarter of the high schools have participated in the introductory course. The project uses district funds and places emphasis on training at the secondary level, technical assistance to building principals, and continued training of elementary teachers.

Hopkins District-Wide Staff Development

Hopkins developed a district-wide program to enable special educators to share information and knowledge with regular educators. The original goals of this strategy were: (a) to help instructional staff develop effective procedures and understanding for the education of handicapped children in the regular classroom, (b) to provide incentives and support for classroom teachers who assume increased responsibilities for meeting individual needs of handicapped children, and (c) to encourage greater use of the special education staff in assisting the instructional personnel in working with handicapped children in the regular classroom.

Two project coordinators worked with the coordinator of special education and with the principals and special education teams in each school to develop learning experiences for classroom teachers. Principals were asked to recruit teachers who had one or more handicapped children in their classes.

Each potential participant completed a needs assessment to identify areas of instruction desired. Special education teachers were surveyed to determine who would be interested in individually teaching or team teaching a session. Participants had direct input into the syllabus of courses. This program was conducted over a two-year period and served approximately one hundred teachers.

The delivery model consisted of an in-service training format of five sessions. Special education teachers and parents served as instructors of the sessions. Eight parents served as instructors, and a number of additional parents observed or participated in the different activities. A total of five days release time was allocated to teachers to attend sessions. Substitute teachers were assigned to their classes.

Four full-day sessions and two half-day sessions were held. One of the full-day sessions was called flexible time. This was a day that teachers were allowed to choose two activities that would meet their individual needs. These included:

- Team teaching with a special education teacher,
- Exchange teaching with a special education teacher,
- Administering an informal test,
- Reviewing test and other data of a handicapped student in the teacher's classroom,
- Meeting with the school psychologist,
- Visiting a district program, and
- Visiting an alternative program.

The other sessions centered on the definitions of characteristics and diagnoses (formal and informal) of handicapped students. Learning styles, curriculum modifications, classroom techniques, behavior modifications, mainstreaming, and current legislation were other topics. Participants completed contracts which included goals for large group sessions and for the flexible day and they evaluated each session.

This strategy illustrates the importance of a significant amount of input from a broad range of persons: the coordinator of special education, project coordinators, principals, special and regular education teachers, and parents were involved. The needs assessment of potential participants increased the relevance of general training sessions and allowed the flexible training sessions to be tailored to the needs of the participants.

Results of the evaluation completed after each session were extremely positive. All the participants agreed that the course was helpful to them. Eighty-seven percent have or will have the opportunity to use what was learned in the course of their teaching. Seventy-five percent felt the in-service training met their expectations and one hundred percent would recommend the course to others.

Minnesota's response to the need to provide training to regular educators provides an excellent illustration of the idea that each school district requires some latitude in the adaptation and use of techniques. Four of the Minnesota districts that participated in this project were involved in the state effort described above. Their individual solutions to the issue vary considerably and reinforce the need to permit districts the latitude to develop relevant programs.

Committee Work

Implementation of the least restrictive environment provision in school districts has intensified the use of committees as an approach to planning and problem solving. Committees may plan staff development activities, create or modify program alternatives, or involve outside agencies in school-community problem solving. The committee is an efficient structure, since it represents the interests of broad constituencies while actually including a limited number of participants in the planning process. Thus, the committee provides support to school personnel by anticipating and analyzing needs in the instructional environment and planning strategies to respond to those needs.

The committee approach used in program planning and organization is one of the more traditional, widely accepted forms of in-service education. As a task is pursued, each phase presents a growth opportunity for those who plan, interact, and decide. Thus, the process of involvement can become an important contributor to the personal and professional gains of participants.

Committee structures for the planning of staff development activities are becoming more commonplace. They promote the commitment of teachers and other school personnel who participate as planners of in-service activities. They also tend to have greater success in accomplishing their objectives than do programs that are planned without representation of the target audience.

Administrative Structure for In-Service Training Programs

In Shawnee Mission, Kansas, district and building-level special education planning committees were formed to coordinate training activities. The district in-service training program was designed to assure:

- That ongoing in-service training programs are available to all personnel who are engaged in the education of handicapped children;
- That regular educators have adequate input into the planning, needs assessment, and implementation of the inservice training; and
- That an organizational structure exists to assure that local building needs will be accommodated within the broad priorities established by the district.

Although over 400 clock hours of in-service training had been recorded for special education professional staff, aides and parents, no district-wide plan of action had been developed for regular educators working with exceptional children mainstreamed in the regular classroom. In an attempt to coordinate in-service activities in the district, a new organizational structure was created to oversee building and district in-service activities.

The key components of the administrative structure of the in-service training program are the district in-service training steering committee and the building in-service training steering committee. It is through the functioning of these two components that the interface between district priorities and local building needs is established. The district level committee was designated to ensure that a comprehensive and broadly stated plan for district in-service needs was developed. Membership is composed of the five area associate superintendents, the assistant superintendent, instruction and pupil service, and the special education supervisor of support services. This committee has responsibility to provide leadership in developing, implementing, and evaluating district in-service training programs. In addition, this committee establishes the budget for in-service training and monitors building-level in service training plans.

The district-level committee designs the broad parameters which guide the efforts of the local steering committees. These parameters include the identification of district priorities, timelines, and evaluation criteria for building in-service programs. Building-level committees generate in-service plans which are reviewed and approved by the district-level committee and the special education area representatives (as described in Chapter 4).

The overall purpose of the building in-service training steering committee is to ensure teacher input into the planning and implementation of in-service programs. Such involvement facilitates individual ownership in the final product. All members of the committee, with the exception of the diagnostic team member, are appointed by the building principal. At the elementary level the committee is composed of the building principal, three regular teachers, a special education teacher, and a member of the diagnostic team. At the secondary level, the composition is the same except that instead of the three regular teachers, the department chairpersons and a counselor are members.

The building-level steering committee has the responsibility of providing leadership in the development, implementation, and evaluation of building in-service training programs. The steering committee is responsible for conducting building-level needs assessments, for delivering or supervising the delivery of actual instruction, and when necessary, for organizing and assisting in the development of in-service instructional materials.

The major implication of this type of organizational structure is the congruence that is achieved between district and local building in-service needs. As a result of this strategy, buildings can develop and implement in-service training programs which are consistent with overall district priorities, but which exhibit uniquely different content, format, or delivery systems in order to satisfy local needs.

Staff Development Advisory Committee

In Spring Branch, Texas, a Staff Development Advisory Committee was formulated to plan general in-service options for district personnel to assess needs and to develop a responsive program for the district. The coordinator of staff development oversaw all committee activities.

A needs assessment survey is administered to the entire staff to determine areas for professional growth. There are separate surveys for elementary and secondary schools. The needs assessment surveys are tabulated within two days. Results are shared with all principals, who may have additional priorities. The district also has priorities and includes courses teachers have not requested.

Coordinators write up objectives and outlines for courses. Instructors are selected from a group of people such as coordinators, curriculum staff, or outside consultants. The course outline and instructor are then listed in a catalog sent to all teachers. Teachers are allowed to register for a maximum of 48 hours. The only other restriction is that their principals must sign the registration form.

An alternative to this process is that coordinators can submit a request to teach a course, specifying a course outline, target audience, and size of class. Requests are usually granted. The committee reviews requests, looking for innovative methods.

Another alternative is that a building principal or group of principals may request permission to develop professional growth courses for their own faculties. These are usually to meet specific needs and are mandatory for the building. Individuals may also request permission for specific meetings or activities. Meetings that have been certified for approval are announced weekly in the *Administrative Bulletin*. Other requests must be made 10 days in advance to the Deputy Superintendent for Curriculum Development.

This strategy offers a vehicle for growth to increase knowledge and instructional efficiency. Many courses in the area of special education are offered. Teachers are not pressured to take courses, but they are available when a teacher recognizes a need for self-improvement.

Mini-Grants for Staff Development

In Hopkins, Minnesota, a committee approach was used to coordinate one phase of the special education staff development program. The mini-grant program proposed to: (a) delegate the responsibilities of assessing in-service needs and for coordinating and providing in-service training in the schools to regular and special education staff; (b) minimize barriers between regular and special education (e.g., philosophical and conceptual barriers); and (c) provide in-service training to groups which have common needs and concerns.

It was felt that major operational changes were needed if the district were to continue providing relevant, extensive in-service training. It was also felt that both regular and special education staff were sophisticated enough to plan, coordinate, and implement in-service training. Local staff would be successful, provided they were offered assistance and financial support from the special education department and the Bureau of Pupil Personnel Services. This belief resulted in the establishment of a mini-grant selection committee with responsibility for coordinating this phase of staff development.

The coordinator of pupil personnel services submitted a proposal requesting funds for in-service activities to the state education agency. These funds were made available through state flow-through monies (under Public Law 94-142, Part B) with the stipulation that funded activities had to promote in some way the implementation of the law. It was determined that mini-grant funds could be used in one of four ways: (a) building-wide in-service training for a blanket need regarding special education, (b) a department-wide in-service training addressing a particular special education topic, (c) system-wide in-service training concerning health impaired students, and (d) specific projects to develop or modify curricula.

Requests for mini-grants are made in writing by any staff member and submitted to the coordinator of pupil personnel services. The request is limited to one page and must include: (a) specific goals detailing what is to be accomplished, (b) plans or strategies to be used to achieve the stated goal, (c) the anticipated cost of the in-service training or project, (d) a justification detailing how the proposed goal is related to special education needs, and (e) how and when results or products will be demonstrated or disseminated.

The formal request is rated on the basis of these criteria by a grant committee composed of two regular education staff members (usually a regular education teacher and a principal), three special education administrators and, occasionally, one regular education administrator. In addition, the committee considers the proposals' likelihood to produce direct improvements or new understanding and their potential for having an immediate impact on the target system or audience. The committee may accept a proposal with the stipulation that modifications such as changing procedures or clarifying specific issues be made. The review process usually takes from one to two weeks.

In general, this process has been effective in increasing the contact between regular and special educators. The overall in-service program has become more responsive to staff needs and the use of a committee has relieved administrators of the responsibility for planning in-service training activities. Grant committee participants have an opportunity to learn skills and gain information while assisting their colleagues in developing a meaningful staff development program.

The three committee structures discussed up to this point have a specific task related to some phase of staff development in the schools. Members of these groups provide a direct service to their colleagues and at the same time benefit professionally as participants in the committee process. Often a committee approach is used to address specific issues or problems. While the tasks of each of these committees varied, the benefits to participants and their colleagues were similar.

Additional Methods for Obtaining Staff Input in In-Service Planning

Four additional strategies illustrate methods of obtaining staff input into in-service training plans. In Dallas, Texas, a needs assessment workshop was incorporated into the staff development schedule. An in-service needs assessment game was utilized in Contra Costa, California, and methods for developing individualized staff development plans have been established in two additional sites. The use of such techniques helps to assure that staff development designs meet both the needs of the district and the needs of individuals.

District-Wide Staff Development Program

Probably the most widely accepted approach to planning and implementing staff development programs is a systems approach. Such an approach typically includes the following phases: needs assessment and analysis, design, program development, implementation, and evaluation. The staff development model documented in Dallas, Texas, is a classic example of how school districts traditionally provide in-service training through use of the workshop. This model highlights the assessment, analysis, and design phases in workshop planning. Dallas' Professional Growth Calendar provides for ten staff development days and eight early release days annually. Five of the staff development days are allocated for week-long orientation and program planning sessions prior to the opening of school in the fall. The remaining five staff development days are arranged throughout the year to provide professional growth activities in discipline areas. The eight early release days provide for building planning and development activities on a program or departmental level.

During the 1977–1978 school year, the special education department used three of the staff development days to promote professional growth in priority need areas as expressed by special education teachers and support staff. The initial staff development meeting in August focused on the identification of priority training needs and suggested learning activities which would promote professional growth in these priority areas.

Supervisory staff, coordinators, facilitators, and outside consultants acted as group leaders for this session. Three 90-minute sessions were scheduled to address:

- Definition of problems of the target population;
- Identification of skills, knowledge, and attitudes needed by teachers to serve the target population; and
- Identification of alternative training activities to meet priority competencies.

Fifteen priority competency areas were identified by personnel working in different instructional settings. Once consensus on priorities was reached, groups identified training alternatives. Instructional groups were divided into small groups of five to ten members. Small groups were asked to identify alternative training activities designed to promote professional growth for each of the 15 priority competencies. Participants also identified a variety of formats (group discussion, lectures, independent study, practicum, assignments, audio-visual presentations, consultation services) and specific suggestions for names of films, readings, and consultants. Following the needs assessment session, a matrix of priority competency areas by instructional arrangements was developed by special education management as a framework for planning future staff development programs.

Planning for the staff development conference days took place over a two-month period from September to November. During that time, conference alternatives were developed and scheduled. Consultants from within the district as well as external consultants from universities, intermediate units, and model programs in the state were identified. The November conference scheduled 65 one-hour alternative sessions; the March session scheduled 60. A conference packet was distributed to participants prior to the session. It included a summary of the needs assessment process, a staff development program matrix delineating the schedule of options by instructional arrangement, an annotated list of options, a personnel scheduling sheet, an evaluation form, a school floor plan, and neighborhood map with restaurant listings.

Feedback sheets provided information from participants on the quality of sessions and the appropriateness of the format and content of the workshops. Reaction to the conference type format for staff development days was extremely favorable.

Using a Needs Identification Game

An interesting form of in-service needs assessment is used in Contra Costa, California. This special education needs assessment is an activity process in which special education teachers and support personnel play the needs identification card game.

The card game consists of a $4'' \times 12''$ spiral bound folder which directs participants to generate areas in which in-service training is needed, prioritize those areas, and delineate the best in-service training format for each area listed. In accomplishing this, each group completes a six-stage process. They are asked to: (a) brainstorm, (b) record in-service training needs, (c) discuss the needs by reading them to the group and modifying them to be more specific or to combine areas, (d) list areas on a chart, (e) post the lists around the room, and (f) lobby or advocate for their particular area of need. Finally, participants are asked to establish the relative importance of each area.

Individualized Staff Development Plan

During the 1978–1979 school year, teachers and administrators developed self-styled, individual plans for staff development. Each person chose a topic or technique he or she felt a need to study or develop which would have direct application in the classroom. Staff used biweekly early release days to implement their plans, and reported overall progress to their principals.

An analysis of the responses to a needs assessment survey indicated that teachers and administrators had diverse needs, with no strong pattern of need by topic. An analysis by school also indicated few strong patterns of need in each school. In addition, administrators were concerned by the large percentage of staff new to the district in recent years and the need to provide an opportunity for those teachers lacking the necessary certification to participate in training to improve skills. As a result, the decision was made to implement an individualized staff development program in the district.

The assistant superintendent for elementary education developed a form for staff development planning. During a staff meeting at the beginning of the school year, teachers and administrators were given the planning form and asked to develop an individualized project for the coming school year. The form asked individuals to specify educational topics or teaching techniques they would like to know more about, specific questions about the topic or technique, and how they would research these questions. For record keeping purposes, copies of individual signed plans were filed with the principal and with the assistant superintendent. On receipt of the individual plans, the assistant superintendent had topics and techniques recorded on cards and grouped by interest area so that study groups could be formed.

The results of the individual study projects were shared with other teachers and with the principal during the spring teacher evaluation conference. In the spring, the assistant superintendent sent a follow-up form to gather feedback about individual studies.

Many of the projects were related to special education. One principal chose to "learn more about educating emotionally disturbed children, which involved a lot of reading, talking with professionals, and preparing a report." Some teachers worked on developing curriculum materials in content areas for their individual project.

Principals indicated that some people "really followed through" and developed "interesting and worthwhile" projects, while others "didn't plan too well" or "weren't realistic about the task they chose" but "indicated that they would like to try it again next year."

This is a rather unusual approach for encouraging people to pursue professional interests. Allowing time during the school day serves to enhance involvement. Corpus Christi, Texas, also recognized the importance of individual endeavors combined with the incentive of release time for their pursuits.

In-Service Release Time

In response to scheduling problems and large audiences which limited the effectiveness of previous inservice activities, the Corpus Christi, Texas, School District designed an individualized, incentive-based in-service program.

A wide range of in-service sessions was scheduled for three district-wide in-service days, 12 two-hour afterschool sessions, and three Saturday sessions. Under this plan, teachers who use their own time to attend either the afterschool sessions or the Saturday sessions are entitled to compensatory time which may be taken during district-wide in-service days. An added feature to this incentive is the scheduling of the district-wide in-service training days on Fridays which precede Monday holidays (when possible) so that employees get a four day weekend. Because of the incentive of compensatory time, employees are willing to attend sessions after school and on weekends.

At the beginning of the year, teachers meet with their supervisors to review past performance, establish professional development goals and select their required 24 clock hours of in-service training for that year. This joint meeting helps to insure that district-wide priorities are considered in the choice of personal goals.

This plan has increased the district's scheduling flexibility and has allowed it to offer smaller group sessions more suited to individual needs. Such sessions offer greater opportunity for participant interaction and allow the use of experiential approaches to the training. This flexibility contrasts sharply with previous in-service sessions in which the large size of the audience made discussion and instructional activities geared to the needs of individual learners nearly impossible.

Pupil Personnel Services

Among the role redefinitions that have occurred in special education in recent years, probably the most sweeping changes have occurred in the school psychologist's role. Traditional assessment and evaluation functions as well as unilateral decisions on special education placement have given way to shared decision making by a team of professionals. Some school districts have sought to involve the psychologist more directly in the delivery of programs and provision of support to other personnel. Worcester, Massachusetts, has developed an interesting approach in changing and expanding this professional role. The Division of Pupil Personnel Services in Worcester has three components: child study, guidance, and special education. State regulations specify ". . . all efforts shall be made to meet each child's needs within . . . the regular program. In addition, all efforts shall be made to modify the regular education program to meet such needs." This provision has encouraged the development of alternative regular education programs within the schools. Responsibility for such regular education programs rests with the child study and guidance departments.

The "in-building support programs" developed by the child study staff are based on the needs of individual schools and are planned in cooperation with school administrators and teachers. A need may be identified by the principal, teacher, guidance counselor, or psychologists assigned to the building. Often, institutions or agencies within the community are involved in planning and implementation. Written plans are prepared, documenting the goals, objectives, activities, and responsibilities of the agencies involved.

Thus the school psychologists are directly involved in planning with building staff, and in most cases consult with personnel implementing the program on a regular basis. Preventive programming has become an accepted practice in the district. Principals and school personnel have responded positively to psychologists' changing role and have capitalized on the expertise these people offer. Members of the child study department report that their department director has encouraged such involvement and enlisted the support of district administrators in these efforts. This encouragement and support is viewed as a key factor in their success.

Summary: Planning Staff Development Programs

This section has discussed several aspects of staff development program planning. The first group of strategies illustrated ways that state policy was implemented in different districts with varying needs. The second strategy groups illustrated the use of committees in planning district in-service training programs. The final group described additional ways of obtaining staff input in planning.

Throughout these strategy descriptions, the use of systematic processes for needs assessment, design, program development, implementation, and evaluation was illustrated. The importance of input from a broad range of personnel was emphasized. The benefits of staff input to this process are many: designs can more accurately meet individual needs and interests if staff are involved in planning, commitment is increased, and success is more likely.

Several mechanisms to assure that state and district policies are considered along with individual needs were described in these strategies. These included proposal review procedures, review of courses suggested during needs assessments and addition of sessions addressing district priorities, dual committee structures (e.g., district and building committees) for program planning, and supervisor involvement in or review of individual plans.

Thus, several major areas of emphasis were illustrated by these strategies: comprehensiveness in terms of staff input, the importance of an expression of commitment from state and district administrators, and coordinated planning which addresses state, regional, district, building, and individual goals.

JOB-EMBEDDED STAFF DEVELOPMENT

There are a number of activities occurring as an integral part of the school day which can result in professional growth. Broadly speaking, job-embedded staff development refers to any activity designed so that school personnel learn with and/or from other personnel within the context of their assigned roles and responsibilities. (This term was developed by Nicholson [Nicholson, Joyce, Parker, & Waterman, 1976.]) This approach is not limited to teachers only; it may also be used with supervisors or administrators. In the process of implementing the least restrictive environment provision, a variety of job-embedded activities have been initiated or, where they existed, intensified. For example, the team teaching and technical assistance strategies described in the previous chapter are examples of job-embedded staff development which allow co-workers to share their expertise. The reader should also be aware that all the consultative functions discussed in the previous chapter may also be seen as a form of staff development. Two strategies which assign personnel to teams for training experiences are discussed here. A strategy to provide consultative support to teachers is also described. A second form of staff development discussed in this section is observation and feedback.

Teams and Consultants

In-house consultants may include other teachers, principals, supervisors and area specialists. The value of consultation is easily understood: An expert can demonstrate or provide information about methods and practices and provide advice and insight. Just as there are many different persons who can serve as consultants, there are many different ways of structuring the practice of consultation. It can be mandatory or voluntary, preestablished or variable in content, at regular intervals or as needed, and so forth. However, consultation requires a supportive social context in order to be successful and should be decentralized and individualized; in other words, it should be client centered.

In implementing the least restrictive environment principle, special educators are often assuming the role of consultant to regular educators. The purpose here is to view consultation models from a client perspective as they function to impart knowledge and skills, while providing support to the teacher working with handicapped students.

Because the maintenance of handicapped children in regular classrooms requires the teamwork of regular and special education teachers, skills in consultation are essential for all educational personnel. The consultant may be a special education teacher, resource teacher, school psychologist, speech-language specialist, other specialist, or principal. Professional growth is inherent in such interactions, for both the consultant and the client.

The importance of ongoing support to regular educators in mainstreaming efforts was recognized by state mandates in two of the states participating in this project. The roles of the resource specialist in California and the generic teacher in Massachusetts were both created to provide an interface between regular and special education in the delivery of service. In both models, the special educator assumed the role of consultant and the regular educator assumed the role of client. Each model had an implicit support function as well as a staff development function. Other consultative and technical assistance roles discussed in Chapter 4 illustrated district or regional efforts to provide support to teachers.

The teaming strategies discussed in Chapter 4 may be seen as providing mutual consultation and support. Other interesting teaming strategies were used in Lynnfield, Massachusetts, and Santa Monica, California.

Cooperative Staff Development Unit (COSDU) In-Service Project

The purpose of this strategy was to increase the knowledge base of regular and generic teachers (this role was discussed in Chapter 4) with regard to learning style theory and to provide opportunities to apply the theory to actual cases. A second purpose was to provide an opportunity for regular and generic teachers to interact and develop strong professional relationships. It was also hoped that through these experiences attitudinal barriers to the successful integration of mildly handicapped students would be lessened.

The Lynnfield school district developed the in-service project in cooperation with Project COSDU of the Northeast Regional Education Center. A planning committee was established which included the COSDU project director, the directors of pupil services and curriculum, and the special education coordinator. During implementation, these core members were augmented by building representatives from administration, regular education, and special education in order to assure building input and involvement.

At the elementary level, the in-service project followed a general format. During the first day of the five-day experience, regular educators and generic teachers were paired together. They worked in the regular classrooms and planned instructional activities for the next day, when the generic teacher would be covering the regular class. On the second day, the regular educators from a single school were able to attend an all-day session at an off campus location. Because only one school at a time attended the sessions, the small size of the group facilitated discussion and interaction.

On the third day, half of the regular/generic teams attended a morning session while the other teams covered the regular classrooms. Then in the afternoon the teams switched roles. The fourth and fifth days were designed to provide actual application of the knowledge and skill acquired during the previous sessions. In addition, session presenters were available to interact and provide critical feedback of the application of workshop content.

Several important outcomes emerged from this project. First, regular educators showed an increase in knowledge of learning style theory and skill in its application.

A second major outcome was the establishment of a stronger personal and professional relationship between the regular and generic teachers. Generic teachers gained a better understanding of what the regular educator is confronted with every day, and had an opportunity to view handicapped students in a different environment. Both professionals, through their interaction, developed personal ties that helped to assure the regular teacher that support and assistance was readily available.

The strategy represents an interesting combination of specialized workshops and on-the-job application of the skills learned during them. In addition, the scheduling provided for coverage of the classrooms without the use of substitutes.

Train and Trade

The major objective of the train and trade program was to improve reactions and attitudes of regular teachers toward integration, through a short-term, multiexperiential in service program.

Based on a review of research on best approaches to in-service, the program was designed to provide individualized on-site instruction which helped to familiarize the regular educator with the special classroom and the handicapped child, while also making special service staff available to further explain procedures and answer questions. Six discussion lessons were developed as the primary focus of the curriculum. These were supplemented by filmstrips and cassette tape recordings. An instruction guide was available for each lesson so that an educator with or without previous background in special education could serve as a moderator and conduct the in-service program. Thus a school principal, the primary facilitator of change within the school, could moderate the sessions without needing previous experience in special education.

The program included a one-day practicum experience after the participant had completed the first two lessons. The practicum experience paired two regular teachers in order to reduce anxiety, and was highly structured in order to provide a full range of activities within a one-day period. The experience began with the regular teachers observing the children engaged in their lessons for one hour. During this time the special education consultant described and interpreted classroom activities and interactions and instructed the regular teacher.

Following the one-hour observation period, each regular teacher interacted with one target child. Teachers gave new assignments, provided verbal and concrete reinforcement, and moved children to appropriate interest centers. The special education consultant who was observing the interactions provided immediate, objective reinforcement.

As the regular teachers gained confidence and familiarity with the program, the involvement of the special education teacher and aide was reduced until the regular teachers were completely operating the entire classroom program. For the remainder of the day, the special education consultant, teacher and aide lent assistance only when needed.

The final activity was the regular educators' planning of the students' lessons for the next day. Following the practicum experience, the regular educators completed participation in the training program by attending the final four discussion lessons.

The evaluation of the training program indicated that a positive shift had occurred in attitudes toward handicapped children. Participating teachers indicated that the one-day practicum experience helped them to crystallize the issues and operationalize practices that had been introduced during the discussion lessons. The brevity of the training program as well as the openness and supportiveness of the special education staff were also noted as facilitating the positive experience. The multiexperiential nature of the program (teachers watched, observed, listened, read, discussed, role played, and worked with exceptional children) also contributed to the effectiveness of the program.

Observation and Feedback

Opportunities which involve systematic observation of or feedback about elements of ongoing activities in school and school-related activities are considerable. Traditional supervisory models are well known, and techniques have been developed to make this a more helpful process. A variety of clinical supervision schemes have been devised which interrelate preobservation conferences, systematic observation, analysis techniques, and critiques of the supervisory process itself. Clinical supervision techniques are developmental in nature. They seek to maximize trust and communication, to minimize personal risk taking by emphasizing goal clarification and sharing, and to use outside assistance to provide action interventions and training, along with clarification and feedback regarding actions.

Six observation and feedback strategies are discussed in this section. Each program emphasizes retraining personnel within existing roles. This implies that the expectations and responsibilities of the role function have changed in some way. The introduction of new systems or processes for delivery of instruction, such as mainstreaming, can have direct impact on role function. These strategies represent effective methods for assisting personnel to adapt to such changes by providing support and skill development. All three models illustrate the developmental nature of this training process and recognize the time required to bring about substantial change. In addition, the models incorporate another feature which is thought to have a positive impact on skill acquisition: the use of peers or colleagues as the primary trainers.

Instructional Improvement Program

In 1977, the San Juan Unified School District in California initiated an instructional improvement program "to help teachers do a better job to deliver the curriculum to students of this community." The district established a staff development department and adapted a systematic training approach for instructional improvement and leadership.

The program was developed in response to a needs assessment which revealed that teachers were concerned with an increasing incidence of behavior problems and lack of discipline, lower levels of academic performance, and a general sense of change in students and the school environment. The district viewed these problems as symptomatic of frustrations with the learning environment and sought to change that environment.

Based on the clinical teaching model developed by Madeline Hunter at UCLA, the staff development program has two major components which involve the training of teachers and the training of administrators. The teacher is trained in a variety of skills directly related to instruction, such as questioning techniques, knowledge of learning theories, a planned program of assertive discipline, task analysis, and lesson design.

The administrator, usually a principal, is trained in clinical supervision, that is, a systematic process of observing these teaching skills and using feedback techniques. The teacher and administrator may then act in partnership, using the same perspective and vocabulary to analyze the lesson, strengthening the weak elements and reinforcing the strong. This systematic model can be described, taught, and implemented by the teacher and, with the supervisor acting as instructional leader, it is a powerful tool for improving instruction.

The program began with the staffing of the project. A coordinator, two teacher trainers, and a materials developer were hired. These positions were filled by district personnel, released from teaching responsibilities by long-term substitutes. The staff development personnel and key district personnel, including the superintendent and assistant superintendent, attended a series of training activities directed by Madeline Hunter at UCLA. During the first year, approximately 130 teachers were trained during five day workshops which were held during the school year and in the summer. Teachers were released from classes to attend.

The superintendent played a key role in involving principals in the program. He called for a change in emphasis and role of administrators from building manager to instructional leader and made it clear that all principals were expected to become involved in training and implementation. The workshop format was expanded to include beginning and advanced courses. Sixty administrators were trained during the summer and six administrators' workshops were scheduled throughout the year.

In order to release principals for training and to assist them in application of the model, interns were used. The district has an ongoing administrative leadership training program (ALTP) which allows personnel in the district to gain administrative training and experience. Fourteen ALTP interns were released from teaching responsibilities for a five month period to become an integral part of this administrative training phase.

During the second year of this program the special education staff used their funds to involve special education personnel in the program. Seventy percent of the special educators in the district had received this training with their school staff.

Initial funding for this comprehensive training program was sought from ESEA Title VI-C discretionary monies in the state. A proposal was funded to pilot the program in nine schools for a period of three years. The funds went largely to salaries and training of staff development personnel and for substitute salaries for training of building personnel. The school board also allocated district money for administrators' training.

A comprehensive training program such as this, which emphasizes upgrading teaching and supervisory skills, addresses many of the concerns which accompany integration of special needs students into regular classrooms. The training better equips personnel to meet individual needs and to adjust to students' varied learning styles. Thus, special needs students benefited from the program. However, when a significant percentage of district personnel are involved in a growth effort of this nature, the benefits accrue to all children.

Secondary Handicapped Children's Model Program

Major organizational changes necessitated by state law and district involvement in the California Master Plan led to the development of this training model. One major staff change was the creation of the resource specialist position. In the large district of San Juan, 75 resource specialist teaching positions were staffed in the first year of participation in the Master Plan. The director of special education indicated that "we picked the most sophisticated teachers to become RSTs and weakened the Special Class Program." Other master plan districts also experienced this problem. This program for retraining secondary special class teachers was based on a variation of the instructional improvement program and represents a bold approach to retraining staff. The intent of this project is to retrain all 22 special class teachers at the secondary level over a period of three years.

The program was developed to address a number of problems in special classes for the handicapped that the district had identified:

- A significant increase in the number of students being referred from learning handicapped classes to severely emotionally disturbed classes,
- A significant increase in the number of behavior problems in regular and special classes,
- Limited positive relationships between regular education peers and special class students, and
- Poor relationships and/or communication between special education teachers and regular education staff.

In order to correct these problems, the director of special projects prepared a proposal which was submitted to the handicapped children's model program at BEH (now OSE) and was funded for a three year contract.

Based on the clinical teaching model used for the instructional improvement program, the training is intended to change both the teacher and the classroom environment. Two demonstration teams, a roving demonstration team and a site demonstration team, are used for training purposes. Each team is made up of an experienced special education teacher and an instructional aide, both of whom are selected from within the district and respected by their colleagues.

Both teams work with the trainee during the eight week cycle, each in a different area of emphasis.

The roving demonstration teacher and aide assume the responsibilities of the classroom teacher and aide for eight weeks. During the first week, the classroom teacher and aide observe the demonstration team. Then they are released for seven weeks at the training site. In addition to releasing the teacher and aide, the roving team has the responsibility for restructuring the classroom environment and instituting procedures to facilitate trainee use of new instructional skills on return to the classroom. The roving team maintains weekly contact with the trainees in order to discuss the progress of individual students and changes being made in the classroom.

The site demonstration teacher remains in his or her own classroom and works in that environment with the trainees. The site teams are the primary trainers and emphasize (a) new teaching methods and procedures, (b) behavior management skills, (c) use of new curriculum materials, and (d) use of new evaluation techniques of self and students. This role embodies both the trainer role and the administrative role discussed in the preceding strategies.

The eight-week training program illustrates observation and feedback in a job-embedded context. The roving demonstration team spends the first week in the trainee's or visiting team's classroom with the trainee present, allowing the roving team to become acquainted with students, classroom procedures, and the general school environment while the trainee team observes.

The trainee team then moves to the site demonstration classroom. The first week is essentially spent observing the site demonstration team and discussing techniques and procedures to be used, including (a) motivation and reinforcement, (b) aides' functions, (c) forms for critique of lessons, (d) the concept of lesson design, and (e) direct instruction techniques.

Over the next six weeks, the trainee gradually assumes instructional responsibilities. Lessons are monitored and conferences occur on a daily basis. The trainee team returns to their classroom and works for the final week with the roving demonstration team on reentry to the classroom and adjusting to the changes made in the environment. Following the eight week session the project coordinator maintains regular contact with the trainee. The demonstration team also receives maintenance training from one of the interns (ALTP) in the district who reinforces their skills in clinical teaching.

Diagnostic Classroom

The diagnostic classroom in Stanislaus County, California, serves as an assessment setting for students and a training and support mechanism for teachers. The intent is to forestall any increases in, and possibly diminish, the number of county residential placements as well as the number of students receiving home instruction. By increasing the teachers' ability to deal with behavioral and emotional problems, the county hopes to allow pupils to be placed and maintained in less restrictive environments.

The program has two major components. First, the diagnostic classroom serves as an intensive, short-term special education setting for students whose primary handicaps are emotional or behavioral. The classroom is housed in a neutral setting that will not be associated with previous failures and is intended to be a temporary placement where students are assigned for less than four to five weeks. During this time, a thorough educational, social, emotional, and medical assessment is made. Total enrollment in the diagnostic classroom is never more than five or six pupils.

In addition, the classroom is a site where teachers are retrained. The project cycles teachers into the diagnostic classroom for an extended training period of four to five months. Over time, this process insures a core of highly skilled teachers for severely emotionally disturbed or behavior disordered classes in the county schools. Teachers work with project staff to implement pupils' programs, and support groups for teachers are established.

The project staff includes two diagnostic teachers, two aides, a social worker, psychologist, nurse, speech and language therapist, and a psychiatric consultant. The project is structured with two diagnostic teachers so that one teacher can facilitate the daily classroom structure and the second teacher can be available to work with newly assigned teachers.

This dual purpose program has several benefits. While the number of students receiving residential or home instruction in the county is being limited, the quality of the county's special teaching staff is being improved. Individual teachers benefit from their upgraded skills, and students are provided with a thorough diagnostic assessment.

Summary: Job-Embedded Staff Development

Job-embedded staff development may take a variety of forms and may involve a variety of educational personnel. Two types of job-embedded staff development were illustrated in this section: the use of teams and consultants and observation and feedback.

These strategies have emphasized the value of sharing expertise among school personnel, especially in light of role changes that are occurring as districts respond to federal mandates. Teachers, special services personnel, and administrators are adjusting to the addition of new functions to their jobs as well as to changes in their employment environment. The conceptual and practical support of their co-workers and the administrative arrangements to provide such support are essential to the success of their efforts to educate each child in his or her least restrictive environment.

JOB-RELATED STAFF DEVELOPMENT

Job-embedded approaches to in-service education are perhaps the most basic; they are, however, only one of a range of possibilities. Job-related training (as described by Nicholson and colleagues [1976]) is closely aligned to professional functions, but does not take place in the context of the job. Job-related strategies such as exchanges and visitations, teacher centers, and self-administered training materials are discussed in this section along with credential-oriented strategies for staff development.

Exchanges and Visitations

Traditionally, exchange and visitation offer personnel the opportunity to observe others in action and see how other schools and programs operate. In addition, they offer opportunity for more substantive interactions between personnel from different schools and districts. Exchanges and visitations may be within the district or may reach beyond district boundaries.

Strategies of this nature may be viewed largely as a means for exchange of information between personnel and indirectly may heighten understanding among those involved. Roles and relationships become more complex as districts work to provide opportunities for special needs children within the regular school setting. Efforts which may assist staff in understanding the responsibilities and experiences of other personnel can be a valuable tool for support and cooperation.

There are numerous formal and informal strategies which could be regarded as exchanges or visitations that have been used by school districts to help personnel gain information or support as they work with handicapped youngsters.

In Arlington, Massachusetts, special education instructional personnel may observe or shadow an administrator for a day. For example, a resource room teacher may shadow the director of special education. This is an excellent opportunity for teachers to gain an understanding and appreciation of another's role and responsibilities on a day-to-day basis.

In California, an example of an exchange at the county level appears most effective. The program specialist from Humboldt-Del Norte was invited to Stanislaus County to share a program which had been particularly successful. A presentation was made and the personnel in Stanislaus County had an opportunity for face-to-face contact with a colleague. As a result of this session, such visitations were planned in several schools.

In St. Paul, Minnesota, personnel may be temporarily placed in another role, usually to carry out a specific function. Staff are attracted to these special assignments for many reasons. It gives teachers a break from the teaching routine without losing seniority and provides a chance to explore new areas, thus serving as a measure to help prevent teacher burnout.

Teacher burnout is an issue of concern as roles become more demanding. Citing the high incidence of teacher burnout, particularly among teachers of the severely handicapped, a number of principals in Madison, Wisconsin, felt that frequent, nonjudgmental counseling sessions were beneficial. As one principal suggested, "counseling these teachers out of special education can be as important as counseling them into it." One strategy, reported by a number of principals, was used to assist teachers of the severely handicapped who found themselves physically and emotionally drained after a number of years in the classroom. The teachers were reassigned to other, less demanding, programs within the building for one school year. Following a year spent in this different environment, teachers were free to return to a classroom for severely handicapped students. One teacher who had been reassigned to another class the previous year reported that this suggestion from her principal was very effective. In her words, "I felt happy to come to school again."

Teacher Centers

A primary innovation in the job-related context is the teacher center. This personalized model may be characterized by what it provides: (a) assistance to teachers when they need or request it; (b) assistance in line with the teacher's goals, objectives, and needs; (c) assistance at the school site; and (d) assistance intended to increase the likelihood that teachers will become self-helpful and independent.

The basic idea is that teachers should be able to go, on their own initiative and at their convenience, to a place near or at their school where they can interact with colleagues and improve themselves at their own direction. The teacher center movement has gained new impetus with the recent federal legislation, and many schools are instituting new centers or expanding existing ones.

As handicapped children spend increasing amounts of time in the regular classroom, resources like the teacher center can be of considerable value to instructional personnel. The opportunity to modify instructional materials and exchange ideas and techniques with colleagues will facilitate the participation of handicapped youngsters in the activities of their nonhandicapped peers.

The Comal, Texas, Independent School District established a teacher center as a resource for teachers. The center was seen as a means of centralizing materials, delivering staff development support, and providing teachers an opportunity to develop instructional support materials. It was designed to operate on a volunteer basis, with materials donated by staff and community, as a minimal-cost resource to staff. The teacher center was also seen as a means of centralizing materials and tracking state-funded educational materials (such tracking is an SEA requirement).

A number of needs cited by the assistant superintendent led to the development of the teacher center. Those needs included:

- Access by regular education teachers to more materials for students with special problems and more professional literature about methods for teaching them;
- Consolidation of material and training resources for bilingual teachers;
- Access to resources, materials, and training in techniques for individualized instruction to acquaint teachers with new resources and materials; and
- A centralized collection of teacher-made material which can be used or adapted for use with other students in implementing individualized instruction.

The Assistant Superintendent for Curriculum took the initiative in planning for the teacher center. The concept was presented to teachers in the district and people were asked to volunteer to help set up the center. A portable building on one of the campuses was not being used and became the site for the center. Furniture and equipment were either located in the district or purchased at low cost. Teachers and principals were asked to contribute books and materials for use in the center. Some materials and equipment were obtained on preview from commercial producers. Other supplies, such as scrap paper from a local printer, were donated by businessmen.

A teacher center advisory board was formed, with one representative from each campus elected to serve. Several committees were established on a volunteer basis to set up and maintain the center. Committees included display, films, publicity, maintenance, and newsletter.

The center was opened in October. Initially, each school assumed responsibility for staffing the center, which was to be opened from 4:00–6:00 p.m. on Tuesdays and Thursdays. Eventually, each principal was given a key and staff could use the center at any time. Volunteers coded materials and developed a catalog for circulation to the schools. An honor system allowed staff to sign out materials.

The teacher center was designed to accommodate a number of resource areas. Areas were set up for filming, viewing, tape recording, and equipment on preview. The subject matter of the books that were available ranged from teacher training and psychology to creative ideas and games for children. Books were shelved and labeled according to content, making it easier to find subject matter. Materials and patterns were at the teacher center to make learning games, bulletin boards, and posters. A roll-laminating machine was available for use. Posters, literature, and complete teaching units were made available on many topics at both elementary and secondary levels. Kits were also available to be checked out. Each month copies of worksheets and ideas for use in the classroom were made available.

Initially, the staff of each school spent an in-service, early release day at the center to become familiar with the resource and work on staff development activities. Later, individual teachers were free to use the center at any time.

Self-Administered Training Materials

Strategies of this category make primary use of mediated instruction, learning packets, and modules. Many are designed to be administered individually or to a small group.

Training materials of this nature have a wide variety of uses; some can be used independently of other activities. Information transmission can be achieved via film, video, learning modules, and other mediated materials. Shawnee Mission, Kansas, had an unusual experience field testing some instructional modules. A federally sponsored project in vocational education in-service training at a local university developed some instructional modules and provided the district with the opportunity to field test them. The modules focused on attitudes toward an awareness and knowledge of mainstreaming, and with minor modification they were suitable for a nonvocational audience. Since the use of materials was part of the project's field testing of the delivery system, the modules were available at no cost to the district.

The in-service modules were developed with certain characteristics. First, they were to be transportable. Second, they were to contain enough information that a group leader without background in special education could facilitate the instructional sessions. Third, they were to emphasize experientially oriented learning. And finally, they were to be reasonable in price. To help lower the cost of the modules, instead of including transparencies or slides, the content for transparencies was printed so that the school district could easily duplicate and make necessary transparencies.

The underlying concept behind the project was that the emphasis should not be on how different handicapped children are and how much the teachers had to learn in order to accommodate them. Instead, the emphasis of the project was to highlight the similarities of handicapped and nonhandicapped children and to facilitate the sharing of the methods, materials, and skills already used by regular educators that would work with handicapped students. Another intent was to provide enough breadth in the 50 modules to meet the many needs of a school district.

A needs assessment instrument accompanies the 50 modules and indicates which module will remediate which needs. Since several modules may address a single need, flexibility is provided to assure some accommodation of learning styles. The package is designed so that each module can be used independently. There is no need to go sequentially through all 50; however, modules concerned with skill development require proper identification of the needs and knowledge level of the learner. The modules are designed so that the leader functions more as a group facilitator than an instructor. Each module contains two 30-minute sessions, and an exercise in practical application is completed prior to the second session so that problems and experiences can be shared by group members.

The experiential approach, the short duration and ample content of the sessions, and the fact that the group leader does not have to be a special educator enhances the use of these modules by regular educators. The emphasis on similarities between handicapped and nonhandicapped students and the sharing of ideas helped to reduce anxieties regarding the task that confronts regular educators who have handicapped students in their classrooms.

Credential-Oriented Staff Development

Until very recently, the most pervasive approach to in-service education has been the orientation toward various kinds of professional credentials. In this context the teacher is cast as a student of higher education, taking courses and perhaps pursuing a degree, much as he or she did in college in the preservice component of his education. With regard to special education in-service training, this is one context where the issue of governance is increasingly in question. Hite and Howey (1977) suggest that in-service education has traditionally been the responsibility of the local school district through its administrators. In practice, however, studies are showing that where universities control the rewards, they effectively control the programs.

The orientation toward college credits is the framework of the teaching profession. Receipt of professional certification and renewal of certification are often dependent on the completion of a course of study offered by higher education institutions, or other courses accredited by school districts or states. Salary increments have been tied to higher degrees. In many cases, state universities offer courses at a lower rate for teachers than for other categories of students. By making them cheaper and in some cases waiving tuition fees entirely, the states and their school districts have attempted to promote professional development along this route. The number of teachers holding advanced degrees is astonishing.

Movement into all kinds of specialties, administration and supervision, and roles as consultants and helping-teachers has been tied to credentials. The result is that anyone who has ambitions beyond the classroom must take higher education courses and organize them along the lines of the degree or credential needed.

Nicholson and colleagues (1976) suggest that what we need are new partnerships, new arrangements whereby the school and university share responsibility for in-service education. Some districts are initiating such programs.

Management Academy

The Management Academy of the Dallas Independent School District was established in 1975 to provide training opportunities for district administrators. The need to provide a support program for administrators was identified by the school board. The director of the teacher center, with the superintendent's support, developed a proposal to address the expressed need. The proposed plan was approved by the school board, which allocated general district funds to establish the program. The academy director reports that in so doing, the district recognized the increased responsibility of all building administrators in meeting the immense challenges of educational management in urban settings.

The target audience for Academy activities included principals, assistant principals, deans of instruction, resource administrators, and interns in the leadership training program. The four general objectives of the Management Academy were: (a) to revise and implement the guidelines for the preservice leadership training program; (b) to implement summer in-service workshop activities for 60 hours, focusing on high priority competencies (one of which was special education) and needs identified by practicing administrators; (c) to offer a series of administrative training sessions during the school year; and (d) to coordinate regular quarterly in-service discussion sessions between the general superintendent and administrative personnel, focusing on current needs, concerns, and problems.

During the first year of operation, the Management Academy used a systematic process of assessing needs, planning and implementing in-service training activity, and evaluating the overall program. The management model which provided a conceptual framework for the program addressed five major areas of administrative competency: management and organization, communication, problem solving, instruction, and three conditions of task orientation.

The Management Academy offers summer work conferences and workshops and seminars during the school year. Some of these courses, aimed at administrators, are required; others are optional. At the end of the first year of Management Academy operation, the program was evaluated to determine the overall effect and the effect of each program of the Management Academy on participants. The evaluation was a descriptive study based on a series of observations, checklists, interviews with participants, and paper and pencil self-report instruments. In general, it appeared, in the words of one participant, that "the training program was beneficial and that the district had made an important contribution by sponsoring this type of training." A recommendation that the Academy be established as an integral component of the personnel department was approved by the superintendent and, consequently, the Academy was instituted as an operational program.

This strategy offers a model for the in-district preparation of administrators for changing roles and conditions in education in general. Least restrictive environment is only one facet of those changing conditions. A model like this one could be modified to address that single facet or adapted to incorporate the LRE concept into a more comprehensive training program.

Administrative Leadership Training Program

The San Juan School in California has a similar but less structured program. The district has an ongoing administrative leadership training program (ALTP) which allows personnel in the district to gain administrative training and experience. The leadership training program is a two year program for teachers who are to move into administrative positions. The interns played a central role in the district's instructional improvement program.

Fourteen ALTP interns were released from teaching responsibilities for a five month period to become an integral part of the administrative training phase. The interns were first involved in training in the clinical teaching/supervision model for approximately one month. Following the training of interns, instruction of building administrators/instructional leaders was initiated. Each intern was assigned to a specific school for two weeks. During the first week, the building administrator was released to attend in-service training instruction and the intern assumed the administrator's responsibilities in the school. During the second week, the administrator returned to the building and with the assistance of the ALTP intern, began to implement the model in the school. Using this process all building administrators were trained over a six month period. Five ALTPs continued in the staff development office for the remainder of the year in order to provide ongoing support to principals and teachers.

Summary: Job-Related Staff Development

In addition to more traditional forms of job-related staff development such as workshops, a variety of delivery models exist. Models discussed in this section included exchanges and visitations, teacher centers, self-administered materials, and district-sponsored credential programs.

Such methods provide greater flexibility to trainees and can be tailored to meet the needs of individual districts. Exchanges and visitations enlarge understanding of others' roles and responsibilities, provide information on the practices of other districts, and can even be used as an aid in preventing "teacher burnout." Teacher centers offer individuals a great deal of freedom in their professional development—they are free to use centers when they wish and to explore topics of interest to them. Self-administered materials offer similar flexibility, and district-sponsored training programs offer the dual benefits of a credential program convenient to teachers and tailored to the district.

CONCLUSION

The Education for All Handicapped Children Act and Section 504 identify the regular classroom as the standard against which to judge the least restrictive environment for placement of handicapped children. There seems little room for doubt that the implementation of these laws will dramatically affect educational personnel roles, particularly the role of the regular classroom teacher. The implications of using the regular classroom are enormous, not the least of which is that all educators—teachers, counselors, administrators, and other support personnel—must be educationally prepared to work with handicapped persons.

Staff development is widely recognized as one vehicle for bringing about and supporting such personnel changes. The mandate recognized the importance of support and training by requiring "a comprehensive system of personnel development." State and local education agencies are responding to this need with a wide range of training alternatives. Considerations related to the selection among alternatives discussed in this chapter are presented below.

Selecting Strategies for Planning Staff Development Programs

Several basic areas of concern arise in planning and implementing staff development programs. These include costs of program development and instructors, scheduling concerns, and coordination and space considerations. The strategies presented in this section illustrated a variety of innovative ways to address these concerns.

The first part of this section discussed the varying ways four districts had chosen to implement state policy emphasizing in-service education. The Mankato district used a regional council to review existing programs, and saved development costs since a program that met their needs was identified. In addition, a train-the-trainers model was used to save instructional costs. Regional and district coordination and space for planning and implementation of the training were required.

In Little Falls, costs were saved by several rural districts which formed a regional cooperative, minimizing their individual planning and start-up costs. In contrast, St. Paul, an urban district, entered into a liaison with the university to develop the district's own training capabilities for building-level programs. Thus, community and regional as well as building-level coordination was required. As the training progressed from courses to individualized consultation and technical assistance, space requirements decreased.

The Hopkins district used parents and special educators as trainers. The program required coordination with parents as well as district and building-level coordination. Costs to this program included the salaries of project coordinators, and since teachers were released from class to attend, costs also included substitutes' time.

The second part of this section discussed committee structures for planning. Committees offer an efficient organization for planning, since few people may represent the interests of many, and space requirements are minimized. Concerns related to coordination and adequate representation, however, are increased.

The staff development advisory committee utilized a survey to assess needs and used paid coordinators and instructors, thereby adding to costs. The minigrants project had advance control of the funds to be used, and minimized costs by utilizing staff to assess needs at the building level, and to plan, coordinate, and implement training, taking advantage of the talent that existed within the district's own staff. This strategy did, however, require committee time for review, and district and building-level coordination.

The third part of this section presented additional methods for obtaining staff input. The district-wide staff development plan in which the district held an initial needs assessment meeting and then designed many small group sessions shows control of scheduling and space usage—the needs assessment was held on staff development days, and the small group sessions minimized space problems. Costs included salaries for coordinators, supervisory staff, facilitators, and consultants.

The Needs Identification Game offers flexibility in space and scheduling and is a low cost strategy, since no trainers are required. Similarly, the individualized staff development plans relied on individual study to minimize concerns related to space, trainer's salaries, and scheduling.

The in-service release time plan relied on compensatory time given on scheduled staff development days, so there were no costs for substitute teachers. This strategy did, however, require administrative time to help plan, approve, and review individual programs, funding for small group in-service training sessions throughout the year, and coordination at both the district and the building levels.

Job-Embedded Staff Development Strategies

Job-embedded strategies minimize space and scheduling concerns, but still require planning and start-up costs, salaries for trainers, and coordination.

In strategies which rely on shared expertise among district employees, such as the teaming strategies discussed in Chapter 4, costs may be limited to those associated with changes in the student-teacher ratio. The idea of shared expertise was utilized in two additional strategies, COSDU and train and trade, which also eliminated the costs of hiring substitutes, since one member of each team could cover the assigned class. However, the specific workshop sessions associated with these two strategies were still subject to space requirements and planning and instructional costs.

The second part of this section described observation and feedback strategies. The San Juan Instructional Improvement Program involved the utilization of interns from the leadership training program to provide release time for principals and substitutes for teachers. District and building coordination was required. Since the actual training was provided at a university, community-level coordination was also required, but other concerns were eliminated.

The Secondary Handicapped Children's Model Program used a roving demonstration team and a site demonstration team. The roving team "covered" and analyzed the class while the teachers and aides received instruction from the site team. Thus, substitute costs were eliminated at the same time individualized instruction to teachers was provided. Space and coordination considerations are still an issue here, but costs and scheduling concerns were minimized.

The diagnostic classroom strategy combines an extended assessment opportunity for students with an extended learning opportunity for teachers. Because of the time required for this training, this strategy is an expensive one, but minimizes space and scheduling concerns.

Job-Related Staff Development

Exchanges and visitations were the first subject of discussion in this section. The costs of substitutes are the main consideration for this type of activity. The new understanding of others' roles and the influx of new ideas they may provide to the district, however, may be of great value.

The teacher center is a flexible strategy, since costs, scheduling, and space concerns can be limited as necessary. Although the center in Comal allowed teachers to visit at any time, the center's schedule can be adjusted as necessary. In Comal, the center was located in a separate building; however, in districts where space is a concern, a section of a library or other available space could be used. Rural districts might wish to use several centers, instituting an interlibrary loan service to minimize duplication of materials. Self-administered training materials are also an excellent low-cost strategy since they eliminate space, scheduling concerns, and trainers' and substitutes' salaries.

Credential-oriented staff development is probably the most expensive of the types discussed in this chapter, since space and salary requirements are high. However, in combination with other forms of training, costs may be reduced by the use of interns to release principals for training as was described in a previous strategy, or by other innovative means.

Such combinations rely, however, on a comprehensive plan for staff development for the total district, which can coordinate programs in a manner that will minimize funding, space, and scheduling concerns. With comprehensive planning and the creative use and combination of new techniques, administrators can help to provide the preparation needed for changing personnel roles and organizational structures, producing benefits that will accrue to all children.

REFERENCES

Clifford, G. J. Issues relating to the future of special education. In M. Reynolds (Ed.), *Futures of education for exceptional children: Emerging strategies.* Minneapolis: National Support Systems Project, 1978.

Hite, H., & Howey, K. R. *Planning inservice teacher education: Promising alternatives.* Washington DC: American Association of Colleges for Teacher Education, 1977. (ERIC Document Reproduction Service No. ED 137 229)

Joyce, B. R., Howey, K. R., Yarger, S. J., Hill, W. C., Waterman, F. T., Vance, B. A., Parker, D. W., & Baker, M. G. *Issues to face.* ISTE Report No. 1. Palo Alto CA: National Center for Educational Statistics and Teacher Corps, 1976. (ERIC Document Reproduction Service No. ED 192 733)

Nicholson, A. M., Joyce, B. R., Parker, D. W., & Waterman, F. T. *The literature on inservice teacher education: An analytic review.* ISTE Report III. Palo Alto CA. National Center for Education Statistics and Teacher Corps, 1976. (Monograph) (ERIC Document Reproduction Service No. ED 129 734)

Timpane, M. *Theories and their application.* In M. Reynolds (Ed.), *Futures of education for exceptional children: Emerging strategies.* Minneapolis: National Support Systems Project, 1978.

Conclusion

RONDA C. TALLEY

The issues involved in providing handicapped children with a free, appropriate public education are many and complex. As was noted early in this handbook, they may be seen as representing a merger of the domains of regular and special education. In order to be successful, this merger must be supported by exchanges of knowledge and other communication, adjustments in personnel utilization, increased use of community resources, and strong, supportive administrative systems.

The field-based strategies presented in this handbook were developed by administrators to solve or avoid problems in local school districts' efforts to meet the current federal mandates. In addition to their potential for use in other districts, these strategies represent principles important to the success of efforts in these five areas.

In Chapter 1, the need for efficiency in making and processing referrals for special services was emphasized, along with methods to improve the efficient use of time and information handling. The section on planning focused on two key criteria: securing input from a broad range of persons affected by the planning, and bringing those persons together for an adequate amount of time.

Chapter 2 discussed three means of resource sharing: cooperative arrangements, interagency agreements, and contracts. The benefits of these strategies were not only monetary. Through them, students received more coordinated services and gaps in service delivery were filled.

Chapter 3 noted the importance of communication with persons external to the school system as well as with those within it. This chapter was followed by one concerning personnel utilization, in which communication support was a major function assigned to newly created or redefined personnel roles. Other functions needed by administrators as they integrate handicapped students included coordination of special education services and materials, coordination of students' programs and the evaluation process, and a variety of forms of instructional support to classroom teachers. Team teaching was one way of providing such support, and paraprofessional aides were also discussed, as they have been used in innovative ways to provide a variety of types of support to classroom teachers.

Chapter 5 described the need for staff input in planning comprehensive in-service programs, and also noted a need for commitment from state and district policy makers. Another point of emphasis was the need for a systematic process for instituting staff development, including needs assessment, diagnosis, design, program development, implementation, and evaluation. A variety of ways to control the costs of staff development was noted.

It is of interest that some of these strategies were combined with other innovative means for addressing particular needs. For example, when substitutes were needed to release principals for training sessions, the San Juan District used interns from its leadership institute, thus providing them with an experiential learning opportunity. Throughout this report, the prototypic nature of these strategies has been emphasized. The strategies may be adapted to accommodate district characteristics or combined with other strategies. It is hoped that administrators will be creative with these ideas, using them as tools for thought in order to develop further innovations.

The interaction of administrative techniques used within a school district is also of concern in strategy implementation. Techniques currently in use in the district may affect the success of strategies newly introduced in that district, and vice versa. Thus, administrators are urged to examine the potential interactions of administrative techniques, not only to search for innovative combinations, but also for untoward side effects.

Efforts to educate handicapped students in most appropriate, least restrictive environments present great challenges for administrative innovation. It is hoped that the ideas described in this handbook will assist administrators in their efforts to provide appropriate educations to mildly handicapped students.

Appendix: Identification of Problem Areas, Sites, and Administrative Strategies

IDENTIFICATION OF PROBLEM AREAS

Several steps were taken to assure that the problem areas addressed in this volume would be those of greatest concern to educational administrators throughout the country. First, the OSE project officer, Nancy Safer, conducted personal interviews with educational administrators in the states of Washington, Texas, Maryland, and Virginia to obtain an initial list of problem areas. Next, discussions with other OSE representatives, SEA and LEA administrators, and special and regular educators were conducted by JWK International Corporation to determine which of the problem areas discovered were considered most critical. Finally, a one-day workshop was held to discuss the problem areas and further refine the list. Forty regular and special education administrators, teachers, related services professionals, and parents of handicapped students from Maryland, Pennsylvania, Virginia, and the District of Columbia attended. Thus, a variety of educational professions was represented in the determination of problem areas. The five areas are: administrative systems for service delivery, community involvement, communication, personnel utilization, and staff development.

IDENTIFICATION OF SITES

Nominations for states and local educational agencies to be included in this study were solicited from a variety of persons with national perspectives of education—representatives of the Office of Special Education, national educational organizations, regional resource centers sponsored by the Office of Special Education, state special education directors, and numerous universities. Discussions with directors of special education in the states nominated produced additional information. On the basis of the nominations and with consideration for geographical representation, the following five states were selected for the study: California, Kansas, Massachusetts, Minnesota, and Texas.

It should be emphasized that this project searched for specific, innovative strategies for addressing five problem areas critical to the provision of a free, appropriate public education to mildly handicapped students in the least restrictive environment. The project did not make judgments regarding the extent to which the public school programs visited were in compliance with the federal regulations of Public Law 94-142 or Section 504, since that would have been beyond its scope and intent. Therefore, the reader should not assume that inclusion in this study is evidence of a state's or district's compliance with these laws. Neither should assumptions be made about other programs or strategies used in any district, since the strategies selected for study are only a few of those in use in any state or district, and others were not investigated.

The following summaries provide information regarding the service provisions for handicapped students in each of the five participating states.

California

California has provided education programs to handicapped children since 1860, the year that the state's Special School for the Deaf and Blind was established in Berkeley. The most recent development in the state's provision of special education services is the implementation of the California Master Plan for Special Education (Senate Bill 1879 [1980]) throughout the entire state. Districts may choose to follow categorical programs pursuant to the statutes in effect during 1979-1980, but they must be operating under the master plan no later than July 1, 1981.

The California Master Plan for Special Education was developed to provide an appropriate education program to all handicapped children in the state. Instead of labeling children by categories, it used the designation "individuals with special needs" for all children receiving these services. The master plan promotes appropriate programs tailored to children's unique needs and aptitudes, rather than forcing the child to fit into existing traditional categories for placement. In this way, the goal of the master plan is to provide services that enable each child to be educated in his or her least restrictive environment.

Actual development of the master plan began in 1972, when the State Board of Education asked the Commission on Special Education to suggest necessary revisions in the special education delivery system. The legislation which made this possible, Assembly Bill 4040, was passed in 1974. By early 1975, the Department of Education had selected six responsible local agencies (RLAs) to implement the master plan. Four additional agencies began implementing the plan in 1976. Assembly Bill 1250 was passed in 1977 to revise, extend, and expand the master plan concept to assure compatibility with Public Law 94-142.

California educators report that implementation of the master plan has offered many challenges. Initial difficulties included finding an adequate number of trained resource and program specialists, designing special education inservice training for existing school personnel, reducing excessive paperwork (due partly to the fact that no one knew how much documentation was necessary), and eliminating the administrative confusion which accompanies restructuring.

The primary purposes for restructuring California's service delivery and classifications were threefold. First, state educators wanted a system of educationally relevant student groupings. Second, they wanted an array of appropriate programs and services. Third, they felt that the master plan would provide a simple, yet efficient, service delivery mechanism with sufficient data analysis, program administration, and public support.

Kansas

Kansas' commitment to exceptional children is longstanding. In 1949, a special education division was created within the State Department of Education. Since that time, the extension of special education services to handicapped and gifted children has steadily progressed. In 1952, 19 classes for the mentally retarded and 60 programs for homebound instruction received state reimbursement. In 1978, 3,255 special education program units for all categories of exceptionality were funded. Kansas stresses the team teaching concept and has developed a number of roles to allow professionals and paraprofessionals to work together to meet the needs of exceptional children.

Permissive legislation regulating the establishment of special education programs was in effect until 1969 when Kansas State Act 72-933 required the provision of educational services for the developmentally disabled by 1974. Special education laws were revised and codified to form the Special Education for Exceptional Children Act of 1974. Kansas State Act 72-966 now mandates special education programming for all exceptional children in Kansas. About 14% of students in the Kansas schools receive special education services.

Kansas' position toward the least restrictive environment mandate reflects a response to the need for a continuum of services. The following service delivery options are offered: (a) home-based instruction, (b) special education materials and/or equipment only, (c) consulting teacher services, (d) itinerant teacher services, (e) resource room services, (f) the special classroom, (g) the special day school, (h) residential schools, (i) hospital instruction, and (j) homebound instruction.

Massachusetts

The Commonwealth of Massachusetts found that their special education programs resulted in disparity in the educational opportunities offered—fewer opportunities were available to special education students in "less favored categories." In response to this finding, a special education law, Chapter 766, was passed. This act was designed to remedy past inadequacies and inequities by defining the needs of children requiring special education in a broad and flexible manner. To this end, Massachusetts developed a system of noncategorical placement through the use of what they term the least restrictive prototype.

These prototypes refer to programs which allow special needs students to be educated with children who are not in need of special education. A child placed in any program prototype is eligible for the auxiliary, supportive, and remedial services provided within that prototype. Thus, the provision of services within a program may be tailored to the child's needs. The program prototypes are:

502.1 Regular education program with modifications.
502.2 Regular education program with no more than 25% time out.
502.3 Regular education program with no more than 60% time out.
502.4 Substantially separate program.
502.5 Day school program.
502.6 Residential school program.
502.7 Home, hospital, or regional program.

It should be noted that each of these stages has a number of subcomponents by which a student's educational environment and service delivery may be described.

Minnesota

While operating under the traditional categories of exceptionality defined by Public Law 94-142, the state of Minnesota implements the provision of a six-level continuum of services. To assist in service delivery to each of the state's 11 special education regions, special personnel called Special Educational Regional Consultants (SERCs) are employed. It is the responsibility of the SERC to assist the state and local district administrators, teachers, and parents in resolving specific problems and participating in activities related to special education programs.

Texas

The basic special education program in Texas provides for the coordinated use of special education personnel, services, and facilities to ensure the availability of a comprehensive special education program for each eligible handicapped student. This orientation includes providing the opportunity for handicapped students to participate in educational programs and activities with nonhandicapped students, thereby addressing the least restrictive environment mandate. The goals of the program include student development, organizational efficiency, and accountability.

In order to facilitate the provision of a free, appropriate public education to students in the least restrictive environment, the state has set up a range of curricular options in which students may receive instruction. These are: (a) itinerant teacher service; (b) resource or team teaching services; (c) homeroom services or departmentalized special education services; (d) separate classes for the severely handicapped; (3) community, residential, and hospital classes; (f) homebound/hospital bedside instruction; and (g) other options, such as contracts with other school districts, regional day care programs, nonpublic school contracts, and state residential schools.

In addition to the special education services provided in Texas by local education agencies, a state-wide system of regional education service centers also offers specialized services. The special education program component of these centers is designed to serve as a link between the Texas Education Agency and school district programs, to provide supportive services and technical assistance, to assure that direct student services are provided to severely handicapped students, and to coordinate regional education services for the handicapped, particularly when such services are provided by other state or private agencies.

Selection of Local Educational Agencies

After states had been selected, nominations were solicited for sites of innovative practices and programs which addressed the problem areas of concern. A list of 70 nominated sites within the states was compiled and ordered by frequency of nomination. The director of special education in each of the nominated LEAs was then contacted by telephone and questioned regarding the strategies, the district's demographic/ethnographic characteristics, number of students served (handicapped and nonhandicapped), levels of funding, and type of service delivery system employed. On the basis of this information, 58 districts in the five states were selected for further investigation. Each nominated LEA was visited to obtain further information on the administrative strategies and to determine the extent to which the strategies could be useful to other school districts.

After the introductory visits, a profile which described each LEA was developed. Information contained in the profiles included: (a) geographical location, (b) ethnic proportions, (c) socioeconomic proportions, (d) numbers of handicapped and nonhandicapped students served, (e) per pupil expenditure for handicapped and nonhandicapped students served, (f) service delivery model, and (g) critical problem areas addressed by district administrative strategies. Based on these factors, 30 districts in the five states were selected to participate in the project. A summary profile of each of the 30 LEAs selected is presented in Table 5.

IDENTIFICATION AND DOCUMENTATION OF ADMINISTRATIVE STRATEGIES

Between the months of January and June, 1979, each of the 30 participating local education agencies was visited for one week by members of the project staff. After an initial day of intensive discussion with top district administrators, three days were used to conduct individual and group discussions with district personnel who were directly involved with or affected by the strategies. Three target groups of persons within each LEA were contacted: those who originated or conceived the idea for the strategy, those who implemented or were responsible for the actual operation of the strategy, and those who were most directly affected by implementation of the strategy. These included LEA central office personnel, principals, instructional personnel, parents, and community members.

Information was collected using a natural inquiry technique in which project staff allowed their discussions with individuals to guide the subsequent collection of information. That is, although a basic set of topics was included in each discussion, the discussion was not limited to those topics. As information on new topics was brought up by local educational agency personnel, it was discussed and clarified, and the new topic was included in subsequent interviews. Thus, discussions were not restricted to a rigid set of topics; rather, as new, important topics came to light, they were discussed and included in the framework for information collection. The importance of a given topic was defined by the educators themselves.

To control for possible bias, two project staff members participated in some discussions. Project staff had received training in natural inquiry techniques and had field tested their use of appropriate discussion procedures during prior visits to LEAs.

Selecting Strategies for Documentation

Within each of the 30 local education agencies which participated in this project, many sound administrative practices were observed. Project staff first considered each school district's general administrative practices which were innovative and successful in meeting the goals for which they had been designed. Staff then considered whether the strategy actually assisted the administrator in implementing the LRE mandate within his or her school district. Many strategies to successfully integrate handicapped students did not directly address the LRE mandate but did result in the provision of a free, appropriate public education to handicapped students, and these were included. Therefore, all strategies contained within this volume assist in the assurance of appropriate services while a subset of these strategies also directly addresses the provision of these services within least restrictive environments.

TABLE 5
Profiles of Participating Local Education Agencies

Participating Agencies	Geographic location			Ethnic group (percent)					Socioeconomic status (percent)			Number of children served			Per pupil expenditure		Delivery model	
	Urban	Suburban	Rural	Anglo	Black	Hispanic	Asian-American	Other	High	Medium	Low	Regular Education	Special Education	Total district	Special education	Regular education	LEA	Intermediate unit[a]
California[b]																		
Contra Region I	X			99	1	1			X			50,000	7,000	57,000	NA	NA	X	
Costa RLA Region II	X			50	1	47		3		X	X	23,950	3,050	27,000	1,561	1,250		X
Humboldt-Del Norte RLA			X	94	1	1		4		X		NA	NA	10,000	NA	NA	X	
Fountain Valley		X		95.5	1	2.5	1	0		X		41,200	4,800	46,000	1,974	1,618	X	
San Juan		X		91	1	4	2	2	X	X		52,000	5,446	57,446	NA	NA		X
Santa Barbara	X	X		67	6	25	1	1		X		12,653	1,347	14,000	2,106	1,865	X	
Santa Monica	X			69	10	20	1	0		X		51,000	3,000	56,000	2,059	1,949		X
Stanislaus			X	80	3	12	.05	2		X	X							
Kansas																		
Central Kansas		X		95	4	←—1—→				X		13,671	1,029	15,700	1,600	2,300	X	
Flint Hills		X	X	90	4	5	.5	.5		X		6,581	851	7,432	1,172	1,400	X	
Shawnee Mission		X		99	←—1—→				X			33,600	3,400	37,000	2,800	NA	X	
Massachusetts																		
Arlington	X			X				X	25	75		6,028	787	6,815	3,373	NA	X	
Belmont		X		99					X			3,630	570	4,200	3,137	1,321	X	

154

Cambridge	X	80	20			X	X	7,350	2,150	9,500	2,412	NA	X
Lynnfield		99				X		2,550	450	3,000	NA	NA	X
Milford		96	1	1	1		X	4,523	500	5,023	1,458	NA	X
Natick	X	97	1	1	1		X	6,093	907	7,000	2,748	1,054	X
Worcester	X	X				X	X	23,211	2,789	26,000	NA	NA	X
Minnesota													
District #916	X	93	1	1		25	40	35	700	400	3,800	4,000	NA	X
Hopkins	X	96	2	1		10	80	10	800	6,881	7,681	1,984	1,650	X
Little Falls		97	1	1		10	75	25	7,100	600	7,700	1,450	1,330	X
Mankato	X	95	1	1	3	10	80	10	6,655	645	7,300	2,512	1,441	X
Red Wing	X	99			1	20	60	20	2,700	480	3,180	1,900	1,095	X
St. Paul	X	80	12	5	3	40	20	40	46,500	4,500	51,000	3,000	1,500	X
Texas													
Columbia-Brazoria		77	22	1			X		2,850	500	3,350	1,500	1,500	X
Comal ISD	X	80	1	19			X		3,605	492	4,097	1,200	1,000	X
Corpus Christi	X	30	5	65			X	X	35,000	5,000	40,000	1,400	750	X
Dallas	X	36	49	16			X		130,000	10,000	140,000	3,000	842	X
Ector County		75	6	18	.5	X	X	X	20,000	3,000	23,000	2,000	1,400	X
Galveston	X	31	42	25	1	1		X	8,366	1,103	9,469	330	NA	X
Spring Branch		98				X			33,800	4,200	38,000	2,000	1,200	X

Note. NA information not available.

[a] An intermediate educational unit as defined by the Public Law 94–142 regulations is "any public authority, other than a local educational agency, which (a) is under the general supervision of a state educational agency; (b) is established by state law for the purpose of providing free public education on a regional basis; and (c) provides special educational and related services within that state." (34 CFR §300a.7)

[b] In California, responsible local agencies (RLAs) are designated to oversee implementation of the California Master Plan. RLAs may represent more than one local educational district, or in cases where a district is very large, the RLA may represent only part of the district.